TEEN POWER Thru CHRIST

Solid Gold Principles and Timeless Truths
from America's Best Christian Youth Speakers and Authors

Ken Davis • Lori Salierno • Bill Sanders
Bob Lenz • Bobby Petrocelli • John Crudele
Eric Chester • Ellen Marie • Doug Herman
Terry Prisk • Jay Laffoon • Laurie Stewart
Bill Cordes • Sam Glenn

TEEN POWER Thru CHRIST

Compiled by
Eric Chester

Copyright © MM

Printed by Patterson Printing, Benton Harbor, MI

Cover design and layout by Ad Graphics Inc., Tulsa, OK
(800) 368-6196

Library of Congress Catalog Card Number: 00-093378

ISBN: 0-9651447-5-5

TEEN POWER™
TEEN POWER TOO™
PreTEEN POWER™
TEEN EmPOWER™
TEEN POWER Thru CHRIST™
LEAD NOW or Step Aside!™
are registered trademarks of ChesPress Publications

Published by:

ChesPress Publications
a subsidiary of Chester Performance Systems
1410 Vance St., Suite 201
Lakewood, CO 80215
(303)239-9999

Additional copies of
TEEN POWER Thru CHRIST
can be obtained from any of the authors.
Contact information is at the end of the book.

Quantity discounts are available.

Web Site: www.teenpower.com

Contents

Introduction

I bet I can list the reasons why you may consider reading this book:

1. You are a teen (or a teen at heart).
2. You know Christ or are perhaps curious about Him.
3. You want more power in your life.

If at least two of my assumptions about you are correct, then this is a book you absolutely must read.

God loves all people, but do you know He has a special love for teenagers? He knows the challenges you face. He knows the pressures you feel. Yet, He wants you to have the power to do great things with the life He has given you. If you doubt it, this book will alter your thinking. If you believe it, then this book will strengthen your faith.

A word of warning before you begin . . . Don't confuse this standard looking book with the average, every day, typical, hooey dooey, garden variety, read-it-methodically-from-cover-to-cover, **keep-it-on-the-shelf** kind of book. Nope. During this read, you can move at your own pace, skip from chapter to chapter, pick and choose to scan sections as you please *and then share it with a friend!* (You'll see what I mean when you finish!)

Teen Power thru Christ is not just one book, but 14 "mini" books written by 14 different authors—including me. All of us also happen to be professional youth speakers. Every year, we address thousands of teens from coast to coast and talk with them about the key issues in their world.

You'll immediately notice how much we differ in terms of our style and pet topic. However, we share lots of common ground, too. We love teens, love Christ and especially love to help teens find their power through Christ!

Because we packed our best stuff into each chapter, this book is loaded with love, advice, ideas, hope, prayers and direction as well as *lots and lots of power!* I could rave on. But instead, I'll just invite you to turn the page and begin taking in the strongest kind of power there is—that which comes though Jesus Christ.

Wishing You Countless Blessings,

Eric Chester

Co-Author and President of ChesPress Publications

Chapter

1

Izzy Reel?

by

ERIC CHESTER

TEEN POWER

Thru CHRIST

Izzy Reel?

by
ERIC CHESTER

O kay, I'll admit it.

I have asked *the question* almost every day. I asked it when I was a first grader at Emmaus Lutheran School, and I asked it again about an hour ago when the cashier gave me too much change. I ask it every time I hear a catchy song inviting me to do something I know is not morally right. And I asked it when the story of the Columbine tragedy first broke. *The question* I ask is this:

"Izzy Reel?" God, I mean.

Is the whole "God thing" a concocted fable like Santa Claus, Zeus, and the stork that delivers babies? Is it just another one of those really good stories used to explain the unexplainable? Is there really a three-in-one being in the heavens who created the universe and all its glory, then sent his son to die on the cross to save us from the evils of our sinful nature?

Izzy Reel?

Asking *the question* causes me to examine my core beliefs. We each live according to our beliefs, so I'm a firm believer that we should at least know what our beliefs are. Because if I thought the answer to *the question* was "no," I certainly would make different decisions than those I do make. I'd *loosen up, get down,* and *go with the flow* more often. I'd *live for today* and *do whatever felt good* at the particular moment.

But I know the answer to *the question.* It's the answer that serves as a compass to guide my actions.

Still, I am human, and an awful lot of compelling information out there makes a thinking man wonder. The clouds of doubt creep up every once in a while when the brilliant people present their brilliant arguments for the other side.

I only wish some sort of universal agreement on the matter would stop the debates. It sure would put my mind at ease. I'd give anything to see the six o'clock news lead one evening with the following report:

> *At 12:43 pm eastern time today, God parted the heavens and showed up in the flesh to grab lunch in Times Square. A stunned crowd of thousands looked on as He healed the sick, turned Coke into Pepsi, and stopped to talk to reporters. He then raised His arms and re-ascended into heaven but promised, "I'll be back before you know it."*

After carefully studying and analyzing the incident, the worldwide scientific community has finally thrown out the ridiculous theory of evolution, and its members are now converting to Christianity. Politicians, atheists, and even Hollywood movie producers say they are now 100% firmly convinced that God does, in fact, exist and that the Bible is, indeed, the inspired word of God.

Full story and video highlights at eleven.

That news would set off hysteria like never before. Millions of people would totally freak out and run, hoping to find a place where they could hide from the very God they had never accepted. The rest of the world would break into a joyous celebration!

Imagine what would happen if everyone alive—the entire population of the planet—finally had the proof it needed to lay all incompatible theories, doubts, and beliefs to rest. Finally, there would be the unquestionable, unshakeable, indisputable evidence of the living, all-knowing, all-powerful God of heaven and earth.

At that moment, people all over the world would have no choice but to live according to what the Bible has always proclaimed:

God is omniscient (all knowing).
God sent his only son, Jesus Christ, to die for our salvation.

We need to love one another, unconditionally.
When we are wronged, we need to turn the other cheek.
Honor your mother and father.
People who marry need to stay married.
Tell the truth.
Don't rip each other off.
Don't kill unborn babies.
Forgive each other, no matter what!
Etc. etc. etc.

WOW! What a day that would be! Peace, harmony, and joy would reign supreme.

If I were God, that's what I would do. I'd come and silence the critics and the doubters once and for all! But I'm not God, so it ain't gonna go down that way. God doesn't play the game the way I wish He would. Even though miracles surround us to prove He is here, logical reasons—and many well-schooled scientists—will argue and contradict the existence of God.

Makes me sad. Makes me angry. And it often makes me wonder why God doesn't just send CNN a videotape of the Garden of Eden—or of the parting of the Red Sea—or at least some piece of conclusive evidence that no scientist could contest! It would make the whole "faith in God" thing unnecessary. After all, no one needs faith in something that has been proven true beyond all doubt.

But as I said, God doesn't work that way. So my guess is that even the most ardent Christians, preachers, Bible scholars, and theologians find themselves—at least occasionally—wrestling with *the question* . . .

Izzy Reel?

Tough question. In fact, no question is more difficult. Because no one can ask *the question* without living according to the answer. Those who answer "no," who do not believe that God exists and that Jesus is Lord, live for this world. Those who answer "yes" put their faith in Christ and their trust in God; they live for the eternity that follows this world.

The In-betweeners

I'll have to admit, I have prejudice in my heart. I have a hard time with the in-betweeners. Those "iffy" people who won't ask *the question* because they fear the answer. The in-betweeners won't deny that God exists, but they won't accept Him enough to put their lives in His hands. They aren't going to kill anybody for fear that God will punish them, but they aren't going to stand up and proclaim their faith for fear it might offend the "anything goes" mindset of the liberal thinkers. The in-betweeners let each day meld into the next, believing one minute there is no God who watches them and the next minute calling on God to help them through a tough situation.

Izzy Reel? Believe It or Not

When it comes to our personal relationship with Jesus Christ, belief is a black and white issue. You either believe in Him or you don't. You either accept God in whole as He is represented in the Bible, or you don't. The Bible does not pretend to be a book of pick-and-choose. You either must accept it in its entirety as the divine word of God, or you have to believe it is faulty. No gray area exists.

Granted, the world often attempts to re-create God in a way that is more pleasing to today's modern world. People often say the Bible is outdated and therefore needs to be adapted to fit the times. Nothing could be further from the truth.

God is very fair, very loving, and very forgiving, but He does not take kindly to anyone rewriting His book. *(Don't confuse rewriting with rewording. Modern translations of the Bible simply make it easier for us to understand His word; they do not change the meaning.)* You see, God knew we would survive into this new millennium, and He gave us a message that would be as relevant today as the day it was written. It's not simple or easy to live according to the pages in His book; in fact, it's far easier to live according to the ways of the world. As a result, you and I are often conflicted, so we must confront *the question* head on.

Izzy Reel?

You and Me: At the Crossroads

Me

A work associate has a hard day and lashes out at me in anger. I protest, *"I did nothing to warrant this. She has no right to speak to me that way! I have the right to be assertive and to defend myself from this unprovoked verbal attack!"* My mind draws upon the influence of the world as I begin preparing my response, thinking, *"I'll just shut her up by telling her what kind of *! ^%#@ she is. Then I'll remind her of the time she really messed up and . . ."*

Just then, my out-of-control thoughts are interrupted. Before I can open my mouth to put this person in her place, I ask myself, *"You know what 'the Big Guy' wants you to do here, Eric. He wants you to lay down your anger and forgive her. Talk to her, pray with her, and help her through the pain she's feeling."*

Yes, of course that is what God wants me to do . . .

All that remains, then, is my response to *the question.*

Izzy Reel?

You see, my answer to *the question* ultimately controls my response to this situation. If I answer "no"—or even if I ignore *the question*—then I take control and do what feels good in the moment, *which is to rip her up one side and down the other!* On the other hand, if my answer is "yes"—

then God is the center of my life and I need to do what pleases Him, not me.

You

There you are at semester's end, studying like crazy for a test you must ace to pass a really hard class. You're reviewing a study guide your teacher gave you when you flip it over and discover that the key to the test has somehow rubbed off on the back of your study guide! Worried about your score, you cannot help but look at the answers. Subsequently, you pass the exam with flying colors. When the teacher grows suspicious of your high grade and questions you on it, you pretend to be outraged at this insinuation of wrongdoing. After all, there is no way the teacher can possibly know you had the key. But God knows, that is, if He's watching? So you ask yourself . . . Izzy Reel?

You go to the movies with your friends, and you each buy a ticket to the light-hearted comedy you told your parents you were going to see. After the usher tears your ticket, your friends duck into the theatre showing the R-NC17 slasher film. It's not what you went to see or even *want* to see, but your friends have all gone inside and expect you to join them. Your parents would be so angry if they knew, but how could they? It's dark in there, and no one can see you—except for . . . well, Izzy Reel?

Your house gets egged in the middle of the night and your parents make you clean it up the very next day. Instead of going to the game with your friends, you end up on the tall end of a ladder washing unborn chicken off your bedroom window. A week later, you are driving home late at night and see the person who you have been told was the "egger." He's stranded by his car on the side of dark road, no help in sight. *"Serves him right, the little . . ."* is the first thought in your mind. Then that inner voice appears flashing *the question* . . . Izzy Reel?

Lying, cheating, stealing, revenge—you and I are drawn toward sin like a paperclip toward a magnet. And whether you consider yourself religious or not, sooner or later you must answer *the question*. It won't go away on its own.

Don't confuse *the question* with guilt, 'cause guilt is an emotion that belongs to Satan. Guilt is what you are overcome with when you know what you should do, yet you do something else. *The question* I'm referring to is simply one of faith. If your faith is strong and you believe God is real, you will chose the difficult right over the easy—and often most popular—wrong.

God never said *"do the right thing if the right thing has first been done unto you."* He never said *"if it feels good, do it"* or *"do what works for you."* Nope. He knew the incredible tests we would confront; He was pretty specific about how He wanted us to respond. Yet, though the challenges are tough, the rewards are great for those who dare to answer *the question* with faith, courage, and honor.

We've Talked About *the Question . . .* So What's *the Answer?*

Yes.

God is real. He is here and He is now and He is everything the Bible proclaims Him to be. There is proof. There is even evidence sufficient enough to quiet the most stubborn skeptic. And although I love it when scientific proof is on our side, that is not what it takes to convince me.

Izzy Reel? Duzzy Kare? Kenny Savus?

Absolutely! How do I know this to be true?

When I look deeply into the eyes of my wife, I see a love that only God could have created. Every time I hear my daughter giggle while talking on the phone with a friend or watch my painfully thin son stuff an entire burrito into his mouth and survive to take another bite, I know God is right there in my home. Each time I ski the Rockies, gaze over the wheat fields in the Midwest, or stare at the sunset over the ocean, I am absolutely certain that these things didn't just happen. When I learn that a fatal disease for which no cure exists suddenly disappears from a young boy's body leaving brilliant surgeons completely baffled, I know it is no mystery; God was there. When I find myself at the depths of depression and fear that leaves nothing but tears inside me, I somehow find the resolve to go on. And I feel God's mighty hand helping me stand to face another day.

I have no doubt that God is real and that the answers to the questions I face each and every day are right there for me in black and white in the pages of the Bible.

Izzy Reel? Yes, and I've bet my entire life on it! So should you.

I say to you, "YES, GOD IS REAL!" Beyond all doubt and without question. God is real and he loves you *as you are*. And whether you've answered *the question* correctly or even ignored it to this point, God loves you just the same. In fact, His Son died for you long before you were ever confronted with *the question*.

The good news is, He doesn't just love those who get it right. He loves us all the same. That bad news is, we're not all in for the same happy ending.

The End Is *Just the Beginning!*

The time will come when God finally decides to quiet the skeptics and settle *the question* once and for all. I don't know exactly how He'll do it, but it's a safe bet it won't happen while He's munching on a corndog in Times Square. When He comes, however, the entire world will know, and every knee will bow and all people will finally realize the true majesty of our Heavenly Father.

Yes, Jesus Christ is Lord, and he is returning soon to this earth to take back with Him to his heavenly kingdom all those who've heard *the question* and have answered the call, *"Yes, God is real and for Christ I have lived!"*

I look forward to seeing you in the crowd on that joyous day. I know you will be among those who are smiling and rejoicing. You, too, know the answer.

May Jesus *Resound* in Your Heart!

by
BILL CORDES

TEEN POWER
Thru CHRIST

May Jesus *Resound* in Your Heart!

by
BILL CORDES

May you live in a way that Jesus will *resound* in your hearts.

Resound? Say it. Go on, say it out loud. Resound! (ri-zound') *1. To echo or be filled with sound. 2. To utter or repeat loudly. 3. To celebrate or praise with excitement.* Resound! Resound! RESOUND!

Of all of the words in the English language, *resound* is one of my favorites. I like the *sound* of it, but mostly I like it because it is one of those words that, when I say it just right . . . *resound* . . . it does just that—it *resounds* inside of me.

Jesus lived in a way that His life continues to *resound* in us. Because He lived, and because we are Christians, we get to feel His presence live in us. Perhaps one of the greatest experiences of being a Christian is having the opportunity to walk in Christ's path, feel His presence, and love others in the way He loves us. It gets even better. Chances are we know other Christians who lived in such a way that Christ resounded in them. As a result, we made the choice to accept Christ into our hearts.

Christianity has been carried, and will continue to be carried, in only one way—by a feeling that *resounds* in our hearts so others can see it. Through us, they feel His love and want to come to know Him, too.

He Walked Among Us

Jesus did walk among us. What it must have been like to experience His presence on earth! Imagine how such a profound presence resounded in His disciples that they dropped everything and walked with Jesus? Here's what the Bible tells us.

> *When He had finished speaking, He said to Simon, "Now go out to where it is deeper and let down your nets and you will catch a lot of fish!" "Sir," Simon replied, "we worked hard all last night and didn't catch a thing but if you say so we will try again." And this time their nets were so full they began to tear (Luke 5:4–6). . . . Jesus replied, "Don't be afraid! From now on you will be fishing for the souls of men!" And as soon as they landed, they left everything and went with him (Luke 5:10–11).*

Choosing to follow Christ means choosing to allow Christ to live in our hearts. This is not always an easy decision. However, we are not alone. Many Christians before us have demonstrated living in Christ and can guide us in developing a relationship with Him.

> *But we Christians have no veil over our faces; we can be mirrors that brightly reflect the glory of the Lord. And as the Spirit of the Lord works within us, we become more and more like him (2 Corinthians 3:18).*

We have all met people whose lives *resound* of Jesus Christ. It is their passion, for Jesus can cause us to want to know more about Him. Christ sends these people to us to help us gain a deeper understanding of Him.

> *I commit to you God, who is able to make you strong and steady in the Lord, just as the Gospel says, and just as I have told you. This is God's plan of salvation for you Gentiles, kept secret from the beginning of time. But now as the prophets foretold and as God commands, this message is being preached everywhere, so that people all around the world will have faith in Christ and obey him. To God, who alone is wise, be glory forever through Jesus Christ our Lord. Amen (Romans 16:25–26).*

People Who Have Brought You Closer

Christ sends people to you from everywhere to help you know His power. You probably have known some people in whom Christ *resounds*. Maybe they had a passion for the Word of God. Maybe they lived in a calm, humble, serving way and it caused you to ask, "What is different about them?" Maybe they were so excited and had such warm smiles that they could not contain God's love—it beamed out of them like sunshine. Their *resounding* faith brought you closer to the Lord.

I have met some of these people, and I am forever thankful that Christ has carefully placed them in my life. They have given me a glimpse of what it must have been like to experience the presence of Christ while He walked on this earth.

Years ago, I got to know a college professor who was different than the others. He could tell great stories, had a kind warm heart, loved people, and was loved in return. When Dr. Jim Costigan walked into a room, the room seemed to light up; everyone around him lit up as well. His presence motivated me to study under him, so I changed my major to Communication and forever changed the course of my life.

Six years after earning my bachelor's degree, I returned to get my master's degree and to study once again under the professor who had changed my life. This time it was different, however. Dr. Jim was not quite as energetic as before. He had cancer and had been going through chemotherapy. His hair was gone, and he had lost half of his body weight. In many ways, however, he was the same. He still warmed a room when he walked into it. People were still drawn to him. And he still had the capacity to make people laugh.

One Thing Never Changes

It is amazing when Christ lives in us. We get to keep all of the great qualities about who we are even in times of struggle. Even though we live in a world of constant change, one thing in the vastness of the universe never changes—God's love for us.

It doesn't matter what storms are storming and what rivers rage around us; when Christ *resounds* in our hearts, we get to keep the good in us because Christ is all that is good. We get to be the calm in the storm and the spark in the fire because Christ is all that and more.

Dr. Jim was that for me—the spark in the fire, the calm in the storm. In addition to all his skills and his warm personality, I grew to understand he had something else. Christ lived in his heart. I guess I always knew it, but during my college years I had drifted away from Jesus (something I don't recommend to anyone). Though I appeared to be having a good time, I came to realize I could only be happy for short periods. But without Christ I was missing the one essential component of life that exists when Christ resounds in my heart—JOY. Dr. Jim had that. And I got to see it firsthand when I found Christ again.

I attended the same church as Dr. Jim and saw how a person could be zapped of all his physical energy but still have compassion and joy. Christ *resounded* in his heart. Seeing him differently, I started to change myself. I started remembering and thanking my parents for raising me as a Christian. Most of all, I asked Jesus to live in my heart so that I could experience the same peace, passion, and joy that lived in my professor.

I was deeply saddened when I heard that my communication professor had passed away. Even though I missed him, I still felt joyful that I had known him. And I was especially joyous because I knew he was with Jesus. Now, Dr. Jim's spirit continues to live in me, through the great memories I have of him and through his teaching. Part of his legacy is that I get to carry on his work of making a difference.

Dr. Jim was good to me and supported me in my speaking career. He encouraged me to pursue my vocation, and his life has given me the faith to push on. I would not be a successful presenter if it had not been for his encouragement.

Resounding Encouragement

In the early days of my career shortly after Dr. Costigan's death, I was asked to speak for a high school assembly in Virginia. This was the last of a long run of speaking programs in Virginia, and the trip had been good. This final program of the week was for about a thousand high school students. It was their last day of school before spring break; they were to get out at 2:15 on a Thursday afternoon, and I had them from 1:00 to 2:00.

The day was warm, and the auditorium was hot. Certainly the last thing the students wanted was to hear a "Motivational Speaker." I was inexperienced, and they were distracted and wanted to start their break a little early. That assembly began as a nightmare. The students were very rambunctious; it got so bad at one point that a student swore at me. That became the straw that broke the camel's back. I stopped speaking and told the students, "I don't feel very respected right now." I began to walk off the stage and instead of feeling remorseful, the students applauded because they felt they had won some kind of a victory by getting me to quit.

As I turned to walk out of the school, the principal stopped me and yelled, "Mr. Cordes, you are not going to leave, are you?"

I answered, "Yes, I don't want to do this anymore."

While he stood there trying to persuade me, I was thinking of all of the reasons I wanted to get in my car and leave. He continued to talk. I knew at this point, he would say anything to get me to go back in there. He said, "You know we have had a lot of speakers here, and you're not as bad as some of them."

I thought, "This certainly doesn't feel very good." Then as I was standing there, I asked myself, "What would Dr. Jim do in this situation?" I remembered that even in the worst of times, he never gave up. Sometimes he would be totally wiped out from his chemotherapy treatments, yet he would still show up to teach his class. I remembered the words he had spoken and how he always had joy in his heart. I remembered he said fear was something that could stop us or that we could overcome. He would say, "Sometimes in life we are afraid, but sometimes we have to feel the fear and do it anyway." Standing in front of this principal in Virginia, I heard the words of my communication professor who had long since passed away. It occurred to me that, in Dr. Jim's words, "In the same way that Christ continues to *resound* in our hearts, we will meet other Christians who will have such a profound influence on us that, in moments of decision, we will hear their voice *resound* in us as well. That voice will be the voice of encouragement."

So the Christian man who had been such a demonstration of faith and hope in my life had once again supported and helped me. I think it's awesome Christ made it possible that others get to live on in us and we get to continue to experience their wisdom and faith even after they have gone. This is inspiring to me:

We get to be the voice that will *resound* in someone else, and that voice, from Christ, through us will strengthen their faith and bring them closer to a personal relationship with our Lord and Savior. Remember, you get to be the voice that will *resound* in someone else!

Defining Moment

Still feeling uncertain as the principal talked, I remembered Dr. Costigan's presence and heard his voice. I felt the power of his faith as it *resounded* in me. So then I looked at the principal and said, "I'll go back." I didn't let the fear I felt overwhelm me. I stood in front of the students and remembered I was not alone. I started talking. For some reason, they started listening. I spoke differently, the students acted differently, and I left feeling as if I had done a good job. If I had not returned to face those students, I most likely would have quit speaking professionally, and I would not be enjoying my successes today.

In that defining moment in Virginia, I learned two important lessons. First, I learned that if someone can push you to the point of giving up, they will take you for a ride. And, second, that when I stand in front of an audience, I am never alone because I have the faith of those who have walked at my side (like Dr. Jim) and I have the love of Christ resounding in me.

I have not walked out on an audience since that day in Virginia, and with Christ firmly implanted in my heart, I never will. Dr. Jim Costigan's *resounding* faith in Jesus Christ spilled over into my life and has given me the courage to face even the most challenging audiences.

Your Faith Resounds. . . *and Spills Over!*

At times your faith in Jesus *resounds* quietly, and some-times it screams from the mountain-tops. Sometimes people can tell by the smile on your face or by the way you humbly serve others. Someday, somewhere, without even knowing that it is happening, someone will feel the power of the Lord's Spirit ringing in you, and *your* faith will spill into *their* heart!

As you continue to grow and to become, many times you will encounter hardships that will make you want to quit. During these times, you must remember that when Jesus *resounds* in your heart, the challenges will not disappear, but you will experience JOY in the midst of the turmoil. These moments will present you with the opportunity to witness your faith in Christ to others and to spill that spirit into their lives. They will see your persistence. They will know there is something different about you. They will know that . . .

**JESUS *resounds, resounds, RESOUNDS!*
in your heart!**

Chapter

3

God Is With Us

by
JOHN CRUDELE

TEEN
POWER
Thru CHRIST

God Is With Us

by
JOHN CRUDELE

"Come on, Peanut," I shout. "Grab my hand!" I reach out, grasp the tips of Emily's fingers and manage to fish her out of a sea of teens all trying to jump on one of the buses headed for downtown Rome—as in Italy.

"I've got you!" I exclaim with a grin while pulling her through the door and safely into the bus. To my relief, her younger brother Paul made it in ahead of us and perched himself on a luggage rack. He somehow slipped in under the arms of the mob. But what about the others? I quickly lock eyes with each exhausted yet still wired teen to do a head count.

"One, two three, four, fiiiiiivvveeeeee," I count, eyes darting around the bus. "And, six!" Okay. My group is all here. A moment later, the diesel engines rev up, and we're off on the final leg of our journey back to our host hotel. It's an exciting time. But as the bus lurches away from the curb, I notice we are so pressed together that I can't move an inch. For the hundredth time today I think, "I must be nuts to chaperone teenagers on an overseas trip! I'm getting *way too old for this!*"

"Okay, God, what next?" I wonder as the ancient ruins of the Coliseum and Roman Forum zip past my tinted window. I feel surprisingly calm. Or is it that I'm just too tired to be anxious? If so, it's a calm by default. Yet, there is a very real, deep, quiet peace inside. Glancing around the bus, I watch the teens trading trinkets that represent their homeland with the other passengers while singing songs in their native tongue. Though it's nearing the end of our eight-day trip, I am just starting to see this group with fresh eyes.

We are pilgrims on a journey of faith. It occurs to me that we are closer to each other as members of God's family than we are packed into this bus. It's cool to know that our relationship with Christ brings us into relationship with all other Christians—from those the Apostle Paul baptized to the teens on this bus from Europe and Asia to our youth group from Minnesota. Our relationship with one another in the mystical body of Christ is spiritually closer than the relationship we have with our mom, dad, brother or sister by natural kinship (John 14:20).

"Well," I think. "This is quickly becoming another moment of profound discovery." Why is it that I need to travel thousands of miles on a plane, transfer to a metro train, and finally board a bus to move the 16 inches from my head to my heart—to understand more deeply how God is with us? Now, looking back on the trip, I feel an even greater sense of His presence.

It's August 2000. Our church youth group flew to Rome to join 2.5 million young people from 157 different

countries—six continents—for the 15th annual World
Youth Day. That's one big spiritual family reunion! Yesterday, we hooked up with everyone in the fields next to
the University Tor Vergata for the Great Vigil. Then, we
crashed for the night in sleeping bags and blankets and
awakened to international contemporary choir music followed by a morning worship service.

Our youth group journeyed to Rome to gather in celebration and worship with a couple million of our brothers
and sisters in Christ at the place of the early Church. This
land is watered with the blood of the first martyrs—the
Apostles Peter and Paul as well as countless others who
died rather than compromise their Christian beliefs. We
arrived in the Jubilee year to walk in their footsteps. We
made this trip to meet God more personally and to draw
closer to the One who passionately loves us—so much so
that He gave His life to liberate us from our sins.

What a holy, history-filled place. In Rome, the Church
extended its commission to carry forth the work of Jesus,
to bring salvation and grace to others even before Em-
peror Constantine legalized Christianity in 313 with his
Edict of Milan. Before that, Christians worshipped se-
cretly, and many were killed for their belief in Jesus. These
early martyrs totally emptied themselves to become fully
united with Christ. Their wordless witness gave us a deeper
appreciation for the gifts of our Christian heritage and
stirred up perplexing questions like, "Would I be willing
to die for my faith?"

One night, Rick Elias and The Ragamuffin Band—in the spirit of its late band leader, Rich Mullins—sang *Awesome God, Sometimes by Step*, and the World Youth Day theme song, *Emmanuel,* from a stage set in the Piazza del Popolo. The words and melody of the theme song lit up the teens and they sang along:

From a thousand paths of light we walk
A thousand miles to Rome
On steps of faith we listen
To the Word which brings us home
Resounding echoes travel
From these walls throughout the earth
The Man of Truth is with us now
And guides us to rebirth

We are here
We stand in the light
Together under the cross
We sing with one voice
Emmanuel, Emmanuel, Emmanuel, Emmanuel

From a city where love poured out
And gave our faith its start
With the Word of peace that changed the world
And filled the hungry heart
We are now disciples
Born again in Him
Our faith is strong, the living Word
Renews and grows within. We are here . . .

Emmanuel, a Hebrew word, means "God is with us" (Matthew 1:23). How comforting to know that though each day introduces us to a new lesson, discovery, challenge, moment of empowerment, judgment, or grace—God is always with us.

While this adventure represented a pilgrimage for our youth group, you don't need to go to Rome to grasp the concept of pilgrimage. Though spiritual pilgrimages may entail taking a trip, the relevant part of faith journeys involves reflecting on the big questions—like the meaning of your life and God's will for how you may live it out. Finding this path is the ultimate joy of living and will make all the difference in the choices you make along the way.

Tourists in Rome pick up things when they visit. They shop and look at the sites, whereas pilgrims divest. They let go of stuff and reflect on the subtle promptings in their heart. In your life's journey, God invites you to let go of the darkest areas of struggle and sin that control you. Those areas may include desires, emotions, passions, thoughts and behaviors.

Remember that Jesus healed the crippled. Where are you crippled in your relationships with others? He healed the blind. What blinds you from the love of Jesus and from understanding and accepting the dignity and beauty in you? He healed the sick. What plagues your soul with hurt and judgment? Jesus chooses us *before* we choose Him. God loves all of you and there is nothing you can do to change that.

When the World Youth Day's opening Rite of Welcome was about to begin, we stood full of anticipation on the square in front of St. Peter's Basilica (Piazza de San Pietro). Various AM and FM station frequencies had been dedicated to air the message in 20 different languages. As our group frantically dug through their fanny packs for their radios, Kelly and Mike tugged at my shirt.

"What station for English? What station . . . " they asked. Scanning the dial, Erin found it first and yelled out, "FM 98.5!"

Pressing the headsets to our ears we heard, *May Jesus Christ, Word of God, who has called you from every continent and invites you to be converted, guide your steps, enlighten your minds and make your hearts pure, so that you may joyfully proclaim his Gospel.*

"What's he saying now?" Mike whispered.

"Shhhh—listen!" spouted Emily.

This is a time to encounter the ever living Christ in the city of the martyrs. You are heirs of a great past. Be not afraid! Open your hearts, lives, difficulties, problems and joy to Christ. Jesus knows all that is inside of you. To serve Christ is freedom. Jesus desires to enter and live in you. He knocks on the door of your heart. Christ is inviting you on a path of holiness to eternal life. Pray together, young people, with the gift of union. Jesus Christ is the same yesterday, today, and forever.

What are you here in search of? Who have you come here to find? Search for Jesus Christ, yet understand that Jesus has first gone in search of you. Celebrate the meeting! God works mysteriously in the situations of your life. You are called to light and are a human person being called to glory. Each one of you are precious to Christ, known personally and loved tenderly, even when you don't realize it.

Let yourself be molded by the Holy Spirit. Ask for the gift of a living faith. Be the saints of the new millennium. Young people, share in the responsibility, and I pray that God will bring your journey to a happy conclusion.

These beautiful, relevant and profound words were shared by the now 80-year-old Pope John Paul II who loves these teens deeply. And the teens could tell. At one point, a boy darted past security and into the Pope's arms. We all watched in wonder as he embraced and consoled the young man. During this tender moment, security knew not to intervene. I looked around and everyone had tears streaming down their cheeks. We each felt the Pope's embrace and understood how united we were in Christ—God is with us.

Whether you're at World Youth Day, at school, with your family, or at church, remember that when people experience the message of Christ, they respond in one of three ways. This held true during the apostles' era, too. Some will look on and scorn. Others will watch and venerate, and another group will follow Jesus and in this way become disciples. In the latter group, the pathway of faith involves three key steps—an encounter, a transformation and a journey.

The Encounter

Initially, encountering Jesus as a friend introduces an individual to the truth. Like any true Christian friend, Jesus will teach you more about how to love, how to be loved, and how to get closer to God. Consider Jeremiah 29:11: "I know the plans I have for you says the Lord. Plans for good and not evil. To give you a future and hope." This hope comes through your relationship with Jesus. An encounter always proceeds a conversion.

Friendships deepen as you learn more about someone, right? So, to love Jesus you will need to spend time getting to know Him through prayer and Bible study. Prayer is solitude wrapped in gratitude. Also, connect with Him through your family, youth group, and church.

Church often gets a bum rap in our society, which glorifies individualism. G.K. Chesterson explained well the need for church fellowship: "People separated from community are separated from God." Your denomination is a family, a Christian community that can present, nurture and protect your faith. It's important to hang out with them if you want to grow spiritually. Why? Healthy families help each member feel loved and lovable. They also discipline, which means to disciple, teach and guide. Guided by the Holy Spirit, they can help you grow in wisdom and understanding (1 Timothy 3:15).

The Transformation

When you give something to God, He transforms it and gives it back to you. So it is with your life. Heavy, huh? As you come to know more about Jesus and what He teaches, as you accept Him as your Savior—a transformation begins and continues. It's a lifelong thing. Author and speaker Matthew Kelley says, "We cannot become more like Christ and stay as we are."

Throughout Christianity's 2000-year history, the Church has transformed pagan places into holy sites of worship. Temples for idols became sanctuaries for prayer. The Pantheon is such a place. Once a site of Roman commerce, it became a Christian church. If the early Church could do this with a building, imagine what Christ can do with your life (Acts 17:23–28).

In the same way, God wishes to make the darkest room in your heart—once a pagan place—a chapel. He wishes to be invited in, to be praised and to light your life from the formerly darkest places. Isn't it exciting to know that God has chosen you, that no matter what has happened up to now, He wants to do many wonderful things in your life? (John 14)

Transformation can be good or bad, depending on what you worship. Remember that you can only become that which is fed into your mind, heart, and soul. For instance, if you take in lots of violence or unbridled sexuality through movies, music, or the Internet, what will happen over time to your soul? Compare that to receiving regular helpings of God's love through prayer, Bible study, the sacraments, and fellowship with other Christians. God's transforming love will help you experience dignity and grant you the capacity to give and forgive and to love yourself and others in a radical way—unconditionally.

God wants to pour out His grace in us, but we too often stand in the way of this gift. Sometimes hearts take a long time to transform from dark to light because God is waiting on you to trust Him and let Him in. Let Jesus into your life, and change will happen day by day.

The Journey

After encountering Jesus and being slowly transformed by His presence, the next step is to make Jesus your Lord. That means moving from loving to serving, from receiving Christ to deepening your faith and bringing Christ to others in how you live (Romans 1:16).

Realize that your lifelong journey may be tough at times. Many new Christians and young people expect their journey of faith to be free of suffering. This natural desire gets expressed through prayers like: "Dear God, please keep my pet from dying. Make my girl/boyfriend like me and not dump me. Bring my parents back together. Get Mom or Dad to stop drinking or being abusive. Please God . . . Are you there?"

God can surely heal these situations. He's God! Yet, if He doesn't change these areas in your life, He still hears you. It's never God's will that you are abused. God gives everyone a free will, and some, unfortunately, abuse their freedom.

On the other hand, spiritually mature people pray for God to be with them in their struggles. They understand that their sufferings may be a joining with Jesus in the Cross. Jesus knows the pain of the Cross and is with you as you face your difficulties.

As the bus weaves through the streets of Rome, I reflect on the closing words of youth pastor Jim Beckman who lost three teens from his church's youth group when they were killed in the Columbine massacre. He passionately challenged our youth to journey.

"You know the truth!" he cried out. "Stand up and be proud of your faith! Get over yourself and be willing to risk and take the special graces from Christ in this Jubilee year out to the rest of the world" (Mark 16:15).

"Hey, here's our stop," I yell as we approach the intersection near our hotel. "C'mon everyone. Kelly, Paul, Peanut—ya got everything?"

"We made it!" shouts Erin. "Get ready to get off. The pilgrimage is over."

"Is it really?" I ask. "Or is it just beginning?" Life's a pilgrimage to eternity and . . . God is with us.

Know What You Believe

by
KEN DAVIS

TEEN POWER
Thru CHRIST

Know What You Believe

by
KEN DAVIS

One segment of the population I have always found intriguing is the "no opinion" segment reflected in national polls. When polls are taken on any specific subject, there is a substantial number of people who are for a particular issue, a substantial number who are against a particular issue, and a small group of people who have "no opinion." They don't know what they believe. I've often wondered what it would be like to be at a party with a group of these individuals.

> *"Hi, how are you?"*
> *"I don't know."*
> *"What did you think of the game Friday night?"*
> *"I don't know."*
> *"Do you have a functioning brain?"*
> *"I don't know."*

The most vulnerable people on the face of the earth are those people who don't know what they believe. I'm not talking about people who are in the process of forming their beliefs; I'm talking about those who are too lazy to think things through and form an opinion, or who just don't care.

When it comes to their faith, many teenagers don't even know that they don't know what they believe. So how do you discover what you believe, and how do you build on that belief to establish the kind of foundation you can live by?

Who Cares?

Why is it important to know what you believe?

Because what you believe will determine how you live. What you believe affects your behavior.

When my first daughter, Traci, was a toddler, I put her into the bathtub and forgot she was there. Forty-five minutes later, I was reading the newspaper when I heard her scream. I ran to the bathroom—and discovered that she had locked the door. Standing outside the door, listening to her screams of terror, I was convinced that she had pulled an electrical appliance into the tub and was electrocuting herself. I broke down my bathroom door to save her life. As I stumbled into the room with pieces of bathroom door hanging from me, she leaned from the tub and showed me her tiny hand, all wrinkled from being in the water. "I'm ruined," she sobbed. It took me an hour to convince her she was not going to spend the rest of her life looking like a prune. What she believed had affected her behavior.

What you believe about God will affect how you live. If you don't know what you believe, you will live an unsure and tentative Christian life. You will be easy prey for those who would like to destroy your faith. Do you really know what you believe, or are you just riding the coattails of your parents' faith? Over the years, I have heard hundreds of students talk about a faith that was not really theirs. They were only repeating what they had heard others say; they had no solid foundation for their own beliefs. There is only one way to get that foundation, and that is to know what you believe and why.

You need this foundation—you need it as much for your own spiritual strength as you need it as a preparation for witnessing to others. When someone asks you why you believe what you do, it isn't enough to say, "Well, that's what my Sunday school teacher told me." Your weak answer won't convince the person you're talking to of anything, and you'll find yourself wondering whether you really believe it yourself. If you refuse to investigate the foundation of your faith, then your belief is reduced to an opinion, and opinions are weak foundations for something as important as faith.

As a boy, I was part of a Sunday school class that had eight students. All eight of us belonged to the youth group and took part in the activities of the church. Each of us had at one time given testimony to our faith in front of the church congregation. Yet today, only two of the eight claim any relationship with Christ.

What happened? What causes someone who was enthusiastic about God to suddenly dump the whole thing? One explanation is that they know what they believed, but then at some time in their lives discovered that what they believed was wrong. Another possibility is that they didn't really know what they believed to start with. Either way, if there's no foundation to your faith, it crumbles as soon as it's challenged. I respect those who know why they disbelieve in Christianity more than those who are too lazy to find out why they believe in it. And I have a profound respect for Christians who have taken the time to discover the solid foundation of their faith.

Believing in Christ is not some wimpy cop-out to avoid facing the real world. Those who have discovered the solid evidence for Christianity know that they don't need to be ashamed to express their faith to anyone.

Here are some suggestions to help you know what you believe and why you believe it.

Don't Be Afraid to Ask Questions

Many teenagers (and many adults) are afraid to ask questions or express doubts because they think that it's a sin or that it demonstrates weakness. That's just not true.

This year I started a project to read through the Bible in one year. The margins of my Bible are filled with question marks that represent passages I don't understand. My plan is to come back later and study those passages to discover the answers to these questions. And they're hard questions—but if I leave them unanswered, my faith will be weaker than if I search for the answers.

Another reason kids are reluctant to ask hard questions is that—sad to say—those questions have seldom been well received. Not long ago, I heard a Sunday school teacher scold a child for asking if Jesus ever went to the bathroom. "It's not nice to ask those kinds of questions," he growled.

After the class, I talked to the little boy. I told him that Jesus went to the bathroom just like he and I did. His eyes got very big and he gulped and asked, "Then did Jesus have parts just like we have?"

Okay, I admit it—he surprised me. But I answered, "Yes, he had parts just like us."

"Good," the little boy said, with a relieved sigh, "then I guess he knows how little kids feel." The boy walked away and left me with my mouth hanging open. Just because someone was willing to answer his question, he had come to an excellent if simple theological conclusion: God knows how we feel because he became one of us.

Just like the little boy, I had wondered many times whether Jesus could really know how I felt, but it wasn't until I had the courage to ask the question that someone showed me the above Scripture. I had hesitated to ask because it sounded so irreverent—and, like the little guy I told you about, I had been scolded more than once for asking the wrong question. But it *wasn't* irreverent. It was an honest question, and I'm so glad it has been answered.

Don't be afraid to ask, and to keep on asking until you get some answers. And don't settle for just another opinion—make sure that answers are anchored in truth from the Word of God.

And that leads to the second suggestion

Learn to Study the Scriptures to Know Why You Believe

From time to time, there have been intelligent people—C.S. Lewis, Frank Morison, and Josh McDowell are good examples—who set out to disprove the Christian faith. They were filled with doubts and questions that they believed would destroy the logical foundation of Christianity. But in their aggressive pursuit of the truth, they found answers to their questions, and those answers convinced them that Christ really was Lord. Rather than disproving Christianity, they became believers. They found those answers in the Bible.

In 1989 a powerful earthquake hit San Francisco, California. Most of the buildings in the city had very little damage because they had been built on solid foundations. Those that were destroyed had been built on landfill. When the earthquake hit, those weak foundations of loose dirt turned to jelly, and the walls came tumbling down. If your faith is built on hearsay and opinion, it's like building without a solid foundation. It may look strong on the outside, but it will never hold up under pressure—which is just when you need it most.

The greatest single thing you can do to strengthen your faith is to get hooked on God's word.

Want to give it a try? Then here's a list of suggestions that will help you search the Word of God for what you believe.

1. *Come to the Bible with an open heart.*

   If the Bible really is God's Word to us, then it's important not to twist its meaning. Too often we read the Bible to find evidence for something we already believe, to seek support for something someone has told us, or to make what we want it to say. Instead, approach the Bible with an open heart, ready to receive whatever it says—even if what it says contradicts your opinions or reconceived ideas. I admit it: There have been many times I have gone to the Bible to prove that I was right about something, only to discover I was wrong.

2. *As you study the Bible, pray.*

   Pray that God will give you the open heart I discussed above, and that you will be willing to accept the truth he reveals. Ask God to take away any ulterior motives and to give you a heart hungry for his truth and the courage to apply it to your life.

3. *Use the Bible as your primary source of truth.*

   As vital as it is to read Christian material and to listen to pastors, youth workers, and other men and women of God, it is also essential that you weigh what they say against the Bible. Many of God's people have been led astray because they choose to believe the messenger rather than the one who gave the message. The more you read the Bible, the less chance there is of being misled.

4. *Make use of other Christian resources.*

   Here are some excellent books to start with:

   Know What You Believe by Paul Little, InterVarsity Press, 1985, is one of the best books on this subject. It is short and easy to read.

   Reason to Believe by R.C. Sproul, Zondervan Publishing House, 1982, is an excellent book that gives responses to some of the objections people have to Christianity. This is a book that will help you know the answers to some of the hard questions your friends and you may have.

Know the Truth by Bruce Milne, InterVarsity Press, 1982, and *Evidence That Demands a Verdict*, by Josh McDowell, Campus Crusade, 1981, are excellent books that cover the subject of belief in detail. They are not easy to read because they deal with the very deepest and most difficult issues of the faith, but they are well worth it. For the motivated student who really wants some in-depth answers they are a must.

All of these books can be purchased at most Christian bookstores. If they don't have them in stock, they'll be happy to order them for you. If you want to really discover the strength of your faith, get those books and set out to find answers to questions like these:

What sets Christianity apart from any other religions in the world?

How do I know that what the Bible says is true?

What do I say to those who claim that it doesn't matter what I believe as long as I'm sincere?

What evidence is there that Jesus really was God?

Is there any proof that Jesus rose from the dead?

Bet Your Life on It

Put what you believe to the test. It's when you really see God work in your own life that the final unshakable touches of strength are added to what you believe.

In college, I was given an assignment to teach a class as creatively as possible. I taught the law of the pendulum, a law of physics that states that a pendulum can never return to a point higher than the point from which it is released. If you put a ball on the end of a string and release it so that it is free to swing, when it returns it can't go any higher than the point from which you released it. In fact, because of friction and gravity, it will fall short of the release point. Each time it swings, the arc gets smaller and smaller until it finally comes to rest. I used all kinds of diagrams, mathematical formulas, and models to teach the law of the pendulum to the class, and I could tell by the look on the teacher's face that he thought I had done well.

When I finished, I asked the class how many believed in the law of the pendulum. All hands flew up, including the teacher's. He thought the lesson was over—but it had just started. I asked him to come to the front of the room and sit in a chair placed against the wall. Suspended from the ceiling was 250 pounds of weight-lifting disks. This was a big pendulum. I brought the 250 pounds of metal right up to his nose and said, "If the law of the pendulum is true, then when I release this mass of metal, it will swing across the room and return short of where I am holding it now. Your nose will still look like it does right now." I looked him right in the eye and said, "Sir, do you believe this law is true?"

There was a long pause as great drops of sweat formed on his upper lip. Then, weakly, he nodded and whispered, "Yes."

I released the pendulum. At the far end of its arc it paused momentarily and then started back. I have never seen a man move so fast in my life!

Carefully, I stepped around the still-swinging pendulum and asked the class, "Does he believe in the law of the pendulum?"

In unison the answered, "No!"

My professor understood the law, but he was unwilling to trust his nose to it. After a short discussion, a student volunteered to sit in the chair. Even though his face contorted in fear as the pendulum started back, he stayed put. But it stopped an inch from his nose and swung away from him again. Now his faith in that law was strengthened. The next time the pendulum swung, he didn't even blink.

When you go beyond just knowing about God and begin to trust him with your life, that's when you really know what you believe. When you trust your nose to what you say you believe and discover that he is faithful, your faith will be strengthened.

And there's no better time to do that than right now.

Butt Prints in the Sand...No More!

by
SAM GLENN

TEEN POWER
Thru CHRIST

Butt Prints in the Sand...No More!

by
Sam Glenn

"We were not put here for 100 years to do, eat, sleep and eat dirt . . . we are here for a reason!" –S. Glenn

Les Brown says, "We were not put here to make a living, but rather to live our making!"

* * * * *

The announcer introduces Sam Glenn . . .

*"Your speaker today is a favorite among youth speakers in America. He battled depression for over three years, yet today is filled with an amazing sense of joy. He went from being a nighttime floor cleaner to speaking for the **Billy Graham Association**. He is author of the book 'Buttprints in the Sand . . . No More.' Weird and wonderful things happen to him all of the time, and he is here today to share some of that with you. So please put your hands together and give a big YAKADOO welcome to Sam Glenn!"*

Sam walks on stage . . .

He thinks—*"What a miracle it is to be here today! If I could only take these people to the days when I hurt so badly, when I battled depression and just wanted to die. Jesus is so awesome! Thank you for being my Hope! Oh . . . great, I have to use the bathroom . . . hold it Sammy boy! Maybe God sometimes calls us to do the difficult things so we can give testimony to His name (Romans 9:17)—Dear God, thank you for this opportunity to share your love, if I should pass out or if something inside of me should blow up, I trust you to get me through this!"*

He greets the audience— *"Ladies and Gentlemen, thank you for allowing me to share with you today. God has an amazing sense of humor . . . just look at me. I'm kidding! Look at each other . . . look at this guy in the front row! Haaaaa . . . let's have some fun . . . we will either make footprints or in the sands of life or buttprints. You get to choose!" . . .*

In a Nutshell . . .

I was 25 years old, depressed, broke, and I slept each night on the living room floor of my mom's apartment. I felt helpless and hopeless. I tried wishing for life to get better, but that never seemed to work very well. I wanted to die! I so desperately wanted to just fall asleep and never wake up again. Believe me I tried that, but always ended up getting hungry or having to go to the bathroom and that just ruined the plan. I had a job as a nighttime floor cleaner, and this was what I had to show for my college education!

This was a time when anything that could go wrong, *did* go wrong. I remember that the day I graduated was a big accomplishment for me. I wanted to do something fun to let the world know that I did it. So, I put white out on the bottom of my shoe saying the words, "I did it." One challenge—I don't spell very well . . . at all. My mission was after they gave me my diploma I would flash the bottom of my shoe to the crowd, they would see the inspirational words and the cheers would come, "You did it Sam!" Yet with the combination of poor spelling and the distant crowd, the words on my shoe appeared to look like the word "Idiot." So that day instead of hearing "You did it!" I heard heckles of people yelling "Idiot!" As I said, anything that could go wrong did. But who would have known that God was building testimony into me, and that one day I would be privileged enough to have the honor of inspiring millions of youth by sharing these stories about overcoming the challenges. Praise God! Moving on . . .

As I cleaned toilets at night, frustration, sadness, anger (and bad smelling fumes) filled my soul—yet I was saved. I had Jesus in my life, but what was wrong with me? Why did I want to die so badly? Why was I so empty? Why was it that everything I did went wrong? Why did I feel like I was the world's biggest nobody and failure? Why had I bought into the lie that I could never amount to anything, or have anything of worth to offer? (By the way that *is* a LIE!) Jesus was in my life, but I failed to believe in His Power, His Greatness, His Truth, and His Way!

The difference was living in a state of fear instead of faith. FAITH, ladies and gentleman is what will activate God's Destiny to become a living reality through you, so that you might be a living testimony to God's awesome power. Amen!!!

The Shawshank Redemption

One night my mom rented a movie for me to watch. I love a good movie. It was "The Shawshank Redemption." A line in this movie dramatically impacted my thinking and attitude about life. One of the characters said, "Life boils down to some simple choices; either get busy living or get busy dying."

Oh my goodness! It hit me like a lime pie in the face. I had been so busy getting busy dying that I had no clue what it meant to get busy living. This was my Shawshank Redemption. The Holy Spirit lead me to open the Word of God (the Bible), and read in Jeremiah 29:11, *"For I know the plans I have you declares the Lord!"* Then it hit me like a pound of cheese in the back of the head . . . **WE ALL HAVE A PURPOSE AND PLAN!!** I am not junk after all. God loves me so much that He took the time to plan a life for me. Then I read in John 10:10, where Jesus says, *"I have come to give you life and life to the fullest!"* He came to give us life, so that we might live our plans and purposes out to the fullest! In a way, it's like Jesus is telling us in John 10:10 to "Get off your puffy duffy and do something with the life, plans, and purpose I have given you! Don't waste it! Go into the world and make footprints in the sand!"

As I gradually came out of the depression, a guy told me that in life we will either leave footprints in the sand or butt prints in the sand. I began to laugh because he said the word, "*Butt*!" It took me a while to get it, but I eventually got it so much that it became my personal crusade! To let people know there is purpose in them. They have worth. We all have dreams, talents, abilities, and greatness just waiting to be brought to life through some ACTION . . . getting off our puffy duffies! *Someone, some where, some place in this world needs what God has put inside you. SOMEONE NEEDS YOU!* You could be a miracle for someone; you could be an answered prayer; you could be the missing link. You could be the only Jesus someone will ever know, see, or hear. It's time to get up and get busy living!

From Floor Cleaner to the Billy Graham Crusade

I began sharing my stories and faith with groups all over. My messages are very joyful, and people laugh until their cheeks hurt and their stomachs can't take it. Yet as I spend time each day getting to know the "ONE" who holds the plans for my life, something amazing happens. *"For you have made known to me the path of life and in your presence you fill me with Joy"* (Psalm 16:11).

Whatever you sow into your life, you will reap. At a time when I was about ready to give up, the grandson of Billy Graham happened to be sitting in on one of my presentations. From there it is all history; never have I looked back, and never has God left my side (Hebrews 13:5). What do you have to lose by trusting in God and allowing His awesome plan to come to life inside of you?

What Will People Remember About You?

Would I come to your funeral out of respect, or would I come running because of what you did in my life and that of others. When people laugh and cry at your funeral it should not be because you are gone or out of respect, but rather because you **TOUCHED** their lives with the plan, purpose, and greatness that God gave you on this planet. You left footprints in the sand . . . not butt prints. **The definition of Footprints in the Sand is the impression or mark that we will leave in the world with the greatness inside us**. To leave footprints in the sand means living your dreams—you tried, cared, got up, didn't give up, you gave life your best and got busy living! To only leave butt prints means you didn't care, you let life and the hard times of failure and unfairness get the best of you. This in my opinion is sad, yet true for so many. This does not have to be. We must not only seize the day but our LIVES.

When my grandfather died, he left a legacy of his greatness. He did not own a huge business or travel the world speaking to large audiences. What he *did* was impact the lives of others in his own special way. My grandfather could walk into a room and light it up. Where there was no smile, Gramps definitely brought an extra one! If you ever got the chance to ride with him in his old red pickup, he would always get you to sing, "You are my sunshine, my only sunshine, you make me happy when skies are gray, you'll never know dear, how much I love you . . . SING IT SAMMY! . . ." He got everyone to sing. He was an amazing man who made footprints in the sands of other people's lives. His passing away was my first experience with death. I didn't know how to handle it, but I witnessed something awesome. At grandpa's funeral people came from all over—some cried; some laughed. I concluded something about life that day . . . that when people come to your funeral and they laugh or cry or try to remember the good times they had with you, it is not because you are gone; it is because you so greatly touched their lives. That is life's great reward.

Remember this: What you do for yourself is gone when you are gone, but what you do for others will remain as your legacy! You were born for a reason. The air pumping through those lungs is filled with a passionate and loving purpose that comes from a living, loving and active God! Remember this always. **Yesterday is history; tomorrow is a mystery; and today is a gift. Seize the day! DO what Norman Vincent Peale says, "Maximize your life, don't minimize it."**

"I Have Nothing to Give"— The Talk with Bill

Bill Leach was a humble man. I met him the day I got saved at an FCA camp in Marshall, Indiana. I will never forget that day—July 29, 1993. First I met Jesus, then Bill. What a star cast lineup. Bill got up in front of 300 young people and did a chalk art presentation. All he said was, "In life you need to have courage," and then he pointed to the sky (God). That was all he said. He then got up to draw a beautiful picture. He had drawn for NFL football teams, president Nixon, and many other groups, but he was a humble man who loved Jesus. His greatest joy was drawing those pictures for four little old ladies in a soup kitchen.

When Bill began to get sick, many people came from all over to take care of him. Before anyone would leave Bill's room, Bill would always ask this question, "Is there anything I can do for you?" He could not even get up out of bed, yet he would always ask that question. One day my brother Ben responded to Bill, "Bill, what can you do for me? You can't even get out of bed!" Bill looked up and said with a gentle voice, "Boy, I can pray for you, can't I?" WOW! We all have something we can do or give.

My dear friends reading this, it doesn't take much to impact the life of another, yet it is in those little things that we make BIGFOOT-size prints in the sand.

God's Weight

We can only do so much on our own. Yet when we take the little we have to help others or impact their lives, it mixes with the BIG that God has and leaves a deeper imprint in the sand than we think—we leave BIG footprints. (Read Ephesians 3:20.) Allow God to fill your cup (of life) every day so that you become a package of hope for someone, somewhere, some place in this world. Let your footprint impression have the weight of God in it! That's powerful!

Remember, God is Watching,
So Give Him a Good Show!

ARE YOU MAKING FOOTPRINTS OR BUTT PRINTS?

Three Teen Power Questions to help you make
Footprints in Sand

1. What do you feel God is calling you to do in life? Pray about it.

2. Is there a mission burning in your heart? Do you feel called to missions, to start a Bible study at school, go to an FCA camp? It can be anything! What worthy cause would you like to get involved with? For myself, I love working with the Make-A-Wish Foundation.

3. What is one thing you can do today that will make footprints in the sands of someone else's life? It could be a simple smile, a hug, a note, a phone call, spending time with someone. What could you do right now? What can you start to do start leaving your legacy of greatness?

Is This Why You Feel Dry?

by
DOUG HERMAN

TEEN
POWER
Thru CHRIST

Is This Why You Feel Dry?

How to Revive a Freeze-Dried Spirit

by
DOUG HERMAN

**"O Lord, I call to you; Listen to me!
Pay attention to my voice when I call to You!"
– David (Psalm 141:1, my paraphrase)**

* * * * *

ave you ever screamed to God, asking Him to answer you? I believe David's throat was often raw from crying out to God begging to hear His voice. David's plea is comforting to myself and to many with whom I pray. We too find ourselves thirsting for God's answer.

My friend and co-writer, Donna Wallace, shared with me a passionate story from her youth. As a young girl, her heart fervently cried out to know Jesus.

> *I remember nights of waiting beside my bed crying out, "Jesus, if you are my personal Savior, doesn't that mean I should know you? Doesn't that mean you should be my friend? Friends answer, don't they?"*

There was a long pause in my prayer. I continued, "So answer me now. I thought I was saved. I'm dying here. I need you now Jesus!"

As I grew through some of those times, my passion never waned. Again and again, I found myself kneeling at my bed with a desperate ache to feel God's presence. I pounded my fist into the mattress shouting over and over again, "God I love you! Do you hear me? I love you." In my breath I'd continue, ". . . and if only I can say it enough times, perhaps even I will believe it and then you will speak to me."

Like Donna, you too may have found yourself calling to God. Perhaps you've sought help from your parish. Your priest or pastor may have offered advice, but it seemed to do little good. You've tried even harder. But that seemed to make the silence and drought more amplified.

For some, God doesn't seem real. Could it be that the question "why?" has haunted you, preventing you from ever coming to Him? Maybe that question has caused you to turn from God—even to the point of disbelieving in a god at all. Have you ever called out to God, only to be answered by deafening silence? I have.

The Power of Drought

Silence hurts—especially when the silence is from someone we love. Though we want to believe God will never leave us, we miss His voice and we find ourselves doubting His existence. In the months following the deaths of my wife and infant daughter, I ached for God's response to my questions. He did answer on one strange occasion—through my lawn!

One summer I installed a sprinkler system to keep our yard green. I love the smell of fresh-cut grass. Being the type that manicures rather than cuts a lawn, I even like the work it takes to make a beautiful yard. Within two weeks of installing the system, mushrooms covered my perfectly trimmed lawn! While great for practicing that golf swing, that was not what I wanted.

"Don't water so much," was the lawn professional's advice. Apparently, over-watering not only causes fungi to grow, but it damages the lawn. Grass requires a season of drought. These dry spells cause the grass roots to dive deeper into the soil in search of water. With deeper root systems, the grass becomes healthier and stronger.

So it is with our spiritual lives. When I sought God and longed for Him to speak to me, I experienced a "drought" of sorts. This silent period of three months caused me to drive my spiritual roots deep into the soil of my beliefs. I began to ask why I believe what I do. In my hungry search for God's existence, I examined all my long-held, innermost beliefs for reality and truth.

As a result, my faith grew stronger than ever before. I knew that what I believed was based on Scripture. My security grew from a relationship with God derived from conviction instead of emotion. Sure, trials and temptations had impact, but with my stronger root system my faith remained unmoved.

My friend, if you feel your prayers are echoing in an empty room, know that God may be using the power of drought to cause you to dig deep into Scripture and into the Rock of your salvation—Jesus Christ.

Where Does God Go In The Wintertime?

Living in Colorado, I get the chance to enjoy those "Christmas Card" holidays. Every year, my family and I trek into the mountains to cut down our tree. At times, the unmarked snow sparkles with such beauty that I can hardly believe it is real.

One year, while taking in this view, a thought occurred to me: "Winter is the season of death." I began rebuking that evil spirit of holiday scrooge-ism when logic pervaded. I've found it's true. Spring is new life. Summer is life fully expressed. Fall is life matured. And winter is life completed—death. But in this winter scene, I was awestruck by the irony of such beauty.

Where does God go in the wintertime? Does He leave His creation to fend for itself? No. We know God is always there. God is not only there in seasons of birth, expression, and maturity. He is also there in seasons of ending, or death. Hmmm, how does that apply to us?

If you are a Christian, you have experienced the wonderful time of spring. New life and fresh revelation encompassed you! Then came summer when you were busy in the activities of your walk with God. In fall, you found yourself involved in forms of leadership and disciple groups. And now you find yourself in winter. You feel dry. You wonder where God is since you sense no growth.

My friend, God is *still th*ere. He has never left you. You have only experienced another season in your journey with the Master. During the times of winter, know this: God is still working in your life. In fact, it is the winter season that causes the roots to become stronger and grow deeper. It is winter that brings completion to an earlier level of spiritual maturity. And it is also winter that ushers in the preparation for another level of spiritual growth! God is about to do something wonderful inside you, and He is using this season to prepare you.

As you endure and prepare in your time of winter, call out to God. Ask Him to reveal Himself to you. He will. But, there are times when His answer arrives unexpected.

Expect the Unexpected: When God Surprises You With His Answer

"Where are we going?" Joshua asked. As a perceptive four year old, Josh knew he wasn't going to the mall or church. The large office complexes looked a lot like those of the doctor's office. And since Mommy and sister Ashli were not in the truck that only meant one thing: *He* was the patient.

I tried to be casual. "We're going to the doctor's office."

"B—but why?"

How do you break the news to an inquisitive child that pain is in his imminent future? I tried to fake him out with a complex-sounding answer. "You need an inoculation, Josh."

"What's a noklaeshun?"

Don't scare him. Don't lie. Be creative. Think!

"Uh. . . . That's a shot, Josh." *Wow, what brilliance!*

Tears flowed freely as Josh scooted his bottom into a protective posture against the passenger door. I tried ineptly to explain the "why" of inoculation, but my reasoning went right over his head. He couldn't get past the needle.

Josh continued his protest all the way to the doctor's office. His cry crescendoed into a full wail by the time the doctor had prepared the needle. It took three of us to keep him on the table.

When stuck with the needle, Josh looked straight at me and cried "Daddy!" In that one word he said hundreds.

"Daddy, why the pain? Why are you letting them hurt me? It's not my fault. I thought you were my father—that you loved me!"

While Josh's face showed pain and fear, I also noticed a startled look of disappointment. I had let him down. My eyes burned with tears as my mind raced to the familiar phrases I had uttered in prayer months before. "Why, God? I thought you loved me!" God spoke to my heart at that moment in the doctor's office. He simply said, "It's the same with you and Me."

A new understanding of *who God is* filled my heart. You see, I love my son. I would even die for him. But, even if I tried to explain *why* he needed the vaccine, he couldn't grasp the explanation. He could only understand simple, concrete concepts. Until his mind matures, he isn't capable of understanding abstract thoughts such as inoculations or eternity. As his dad, my heart cried out to him in his pain. I ached to help him understand that I loved him even though I was helping cause the pain.

So it is with our heavenly Father. While we can handle some complex thoughts, God is *all*-knowing! His level of thought so exceeds our own that we can never fully understand the reasons God acts as He does. I believe that if He could explain all the answers to our questions, He would. However, the answers would probably zip over our heads and we would label them "illogical." We just wouldn't get it. You see, many circumstances in life are senseless from our perspective. But that does not mean that God does not love us. He does. So much so, that He died for us.

I picked up Josh and held him. "It's okay, Josh. Daddy loves you." With every word I said to Josh, I could see the tear-stained face of God reassuring me of His love for me. I hugged Joshua and sensed God holding me and stroking my wounded soul. And I realized that it was not the "why" that was important, but the "who" and the "where" of my relationship with Josh. Who? He was my son. Where? I was *with* him. God too is your loving father, and *He is with you* right now.

It was then that my faith matured deeply. I knew I was going to make it. While there was much I did not understand, I knew God loved me. His heart was set on my good—even when the events in my life seemed illogical. In our trials we can draw nearer to the heart of God and *there* we will find hope.

Confirmed Strength

In *The Screwtape Letters*, C.S. Lewis shows the demon Screwtape giving warning to his nephew, Wormwood. Wormwood is trying to lure a newborn Christian away from the church. Screwtape directs, "If once they get through this initial dryness successfully, they become much less dependent on emotion and therefore much harder to tempt."

Remember this my friend. That even during dry seasons, our lives can still be effective. God still honors our prayers—even when we don't "feel" it. Sometimes it requires greater faith to pray without feeling the presence of God. But when we come through it, we are stronger. Listen, it is the very fact that you *are* dry that causes you to thirst for God. Thirsting for your Savior is not a signal of your sickness but of your health.

Little did Donna know that even as a young girl, God was with her, holding her in the quiet darkness. God allowed her desire for His presence to take root and grow. This was vital, so that He could lead her on a journey of knowing Him. Trust God in the dry, cool place. He is there with you. He is loving and strong—although silent at times. And, He is waiting for your call.

> *"We have only to want Him now at this moment— and at any moment in our lives—and He is there, wanting us, longing to welcome us, to forgive us all that has gone before that has separated us from Him. 'If anyone loves me he will keep my word, and My Father will love him, and we shall come to him and make our home with him' (John 14:23). God makes his home in you. They are not empty words. It is true. 'Make your home in me, as I make mine in you.'"*— (From <u>Prayer</u> by Mother Frances Dominica)

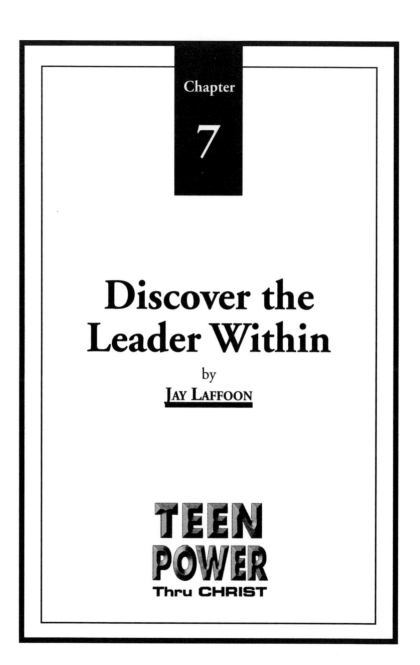

Chapter

7

Discover the Leader Within

by
JAY LAFFOON

TEEN POWER
Thru CHRIST

Discover the Leader Within

by

JAY LAFFOON

I f a three year old can be a leader, anyone can.

The fact that the children were all sitting quietly on the floor was a miracle in itself. There was a bit of motivation however; the occasion was a birthday party. The cake and ice cream were being sliced and scooped in very large portions, and the little munchkins could hardly wait for the last person to be served, so they could begin to enjoy the feast.

As soon as the last child's bowl hit the floor, little Grace the birthday girl exclaimed, "Wait! We have to pray before we eat." She held out her hands to the children on either side of her. All the children clasped hands and formed a neatly bunched circle on the floor. Grace began to pray, *"Dear Jesus, thank you for this day, thank you that my friends could come to my birthday party, and thank you for all my presents and the cake and ice cream too. Amen!"*

Every adult in the room fell silent as little three-year-old Grace led us so simply. The role of leader that day was not filled by Mom or Dad, not by the pastor or his wife who were attending the party, nor by any other adult in the room. Little Grace had taken that moment to show everyone that leadership is not about power, position, or prestige. Leadership is about influencing people. Grace had done what some would say impossible: a three-year-old leading children and adults alike.

General Colin Powell sums it up best. *"Leadership is the art of doing what the science of management says is impossible!"* That's right, when you discover the leader within, you will begin to do what others have said is impossible. The dreams you dare to dream, the secret desires of your heart, and the goals you once thought impossible will take shape before your eyes. As the age old proverb goes "Shoot for the stars, and you may land on the moon!"

Let's discover the leader within! Carefully read the following passage of scripture; it contains the three keys for discovering the leader within.

> *Therefore, since we are surrounded by such a great cloud of witnesses, let us throw off everything that hinders and the sin that so easily entangles, and let us run with perseverance the race marked out for us. Let us fix our eyes on Jesus, the author and perfecter of our faith . . .* – (Hebrews 12:1, 2, NIV).

They're watching!
Take a close look at the first part of that verse. Have you ever felt as though someone was "watching you"? We are

surrounded by many people who are watching us. Friends look to see how we relate to the people we come in contact with. Parents want to see how we respond to the increased responsibilities of growing up. Teachers watch to learn how we react to assignments, tests, and quizzes. It's all part of the world we live in; people are watching!

If that's not enough, look at all the people listed in Hebrews 11: Noah, Abraham, Moses, David, just to name a few. They're in heaven, along with grandmas and grandpas, aunts, uncles, and other loved ones who are "watching" us as we walk through this life.

Expect Excellence

The first key for discovering the leader within is to EXPECT EXCELLENCE. The Hebrews passage states, *"throw off everything that hinders and the sin that so easily entangles."* Putting that another way, it means EXPECT EXCELLENCE. The image the writer is using here is that of an ancient Greek marathon runner. In ancient Greece, the marathon runners would literally run naked. Do that today, and you'll get arrested. Their theory was that any stitch of clothing left on the body could going to keep them from running their fastest, so they took it all off. If you are to become the leader God intends you to be you must be willing to throw off anything that could slow you down.

In the movie "Dead Poets Society," Robin Williams plays a slightly eccentric teacher in a posh all boys' school. One day he takes his class into the hallway and has the boys examine pictures on the walls of past graduating classes. As the boys looked at the photos, Williams says; "Look into their eyes. They all had the same dreams and goals as you, but now they all have one thing in common . . . they're pushing up daisies, they're all dead!"

The boys didn't know what to make of their teachers odd statement. Then Williams continues, "But if you listen very close, you can hear their legacy . . . " The music begins to swell; the camera focuses on the boys as they lean closer to the pictures, and in the background Robin Williams say in an eerie voice, "Carpe Diem . . . Carpe Diem, Seize the Day, Seize the Day, boys!"

Expecting excellence is nothing more than *seizing the day*. This means throwing off those things that keep us from doing our best. We live in a world where we think we have to be "The Best" We watch athletes who are the best and movies where the actors look the best, and we believe that if we don't look or act like them then we just don't measure up. Don't compare yourself to them. Instead, look at yourself and ask: Have I given *my* best?

Next, let's look at the phrase, *"The sin that so easily entangles."* People in ancient Greece wore sandals with long leather straps. Those straps would wrap many times around the calf and tie at the knee. If a someone tried to run in his sandals, the straps would come undone and would begin to flop around his legs. Before he knew it the straps would get entangled in his legs and trip him up.

What a great picture for us. So often we don't see our sin as all that bad. We rationalize, "I'm not hurting anyone, so what's the problem?" The problem is that sin in left untreated will ultimately entangle us and keep us from finishing the race. So, throw it off, and when you do, be sure to throw it at the cross of Jesus—that's where it belongs. Expect excellence of yourself daily, and you will begin to, *Discover the leader within*!

Commit to Consistency

The second key for discovering the leader within is to COMMIT TO CONSISTENCY. This means running *"with perseverance the race marked out for us."* Again the image is of a marathon runner. Life is not a sprint; it's a marathon. That's an important point to remember. One of the character traits needed to run a marathon is perseverance. In order to complete the grueling 26 miles 385 yards of a marathon, a runner needs to persevere. In the same way, in order to complete the grueling tests of life, a person needs to persevere.

If you love music of any kind, you need to do yourself a favor and listen to the most beautiful voice in the world. Beverly Sills has what has been called the finest voice America has ever produced. Now understand, Beverly Sills sings Opera. Okay, so you don't normally listen to opera.

In fact, you may not even like listening to men in tights singing in foreign languages. But if you truly love great music, you need to hear this woman sing.

Known as "America's Greatest Opera Star," Beverly Sills is the Michael Jordan or Tiger Woods or Bill Gates of opera. Simply put, she is the greatest! Beverly Sills was once asked how she had become so great, had achieved so much? She answered, *"Frankly, I don't know . . . but I do know that there are no short cuts to anyplace worth going!"* She became the best in her field because she understood the value of perseverance.

We live in the land of the instant on TV, the age of the microwave oven that will cook a meal in minutes, and the time in history where the lottery means you can become a multi-millionaire with the choice of a number. What do you mean no short cuts? Just that—there are no shortcuts to becoming the leader God wants you to be. The second key for discovering the leader within is to commit to consistency in everything you do.

Be Founded in Faith

The final key for discovering the leader within is, to BE FOUNDED IN FAITH. Hebrews implores, *"Let us fix our eyes on Jesus, the author and perfecter of our faith."* It is imperative as we grow in our leadership that we keep our eyes in the right place.

In order to have faith, you must believe. The word believe actually comes from the ancient Greek, and it means "**to live by.**" To the people who lived in the time of the Bible, this word, believe, had tremendous meaning. It meant a lot to say that you believed in something, because it meant you were not only willing to live by what you said you believed, it you also were willing to die by what you believed.

Unfortunately today, the word believe has become watered down. These days, it has about the same meaning as the word opinion. For example, someone might say, "I *believe* Pizza Hut is better than Dominos" or "I *believe* Ford is better than Chevy." Opinions are like armpits. We all have two, and they generally stink!

In order to truly believe in something you must have faith; the two go hand in hand. Os Guinness says, *"Without faith in the future there is no power for the present."* Perhaps that's why the world has so many powerless leaders today. Perhaps that is why we are in such desperate need for authentic leadership. No doubt faith is what is necessary to become the leader God wants you to be. You must put your faith, your belief, in something or someone worth living for, and ultimately, something or someone worth dying for.

Jesus Christ said, *"I am the way the truth and the life, no one comes to the Father except through me."* Those are pretty strong words. If Jesus is the only way, then He is the only one worth believing in. He is the foundation of our faith and is truly the ultimate person worth living, and dying for. Before you can ultimately, discover the leader within, you must be founded in faith.

The Pin

My dad taught me the greatest lesson on leadership I have ever learned. A number of years ago my mom slipped and fell on the ice breaking her right leg in ten different spots between her knee and her ankle. The doctors said that as little as ten years earlier they would have had to amputate her leg because the break was so severe.

They put my mom in a devise called a Minnelli-Spinnelli. Basically, they drilled surgical steel pins through my mom's leg sideways. The pins went through her leg, through one of the bone pieces and out the other side of her leg. These pins were attached to one of the two metal plates, which went around her leg, one near the ankle, and the other near her knee. Her leg looked like something out of a sci-fi movie!

The doctor said that mom would be lucky to ever be able to walk again without the aid of a cane or a walker. The doctor told my dad that he would play a key role in mom's recovery. His job was to clean the sites where the pins came out of the leg—14 places.

Every morning dad would get up early in order to start the cleaning process. That's where he showed me what it meant to EXPECT EXCELLENCE. He got down on his hands and knees, with two bright lights shining down on mom's leg, in order to begin.

First, he took a solution to break away the scab that had formed around each pin-site. Then, he took an antiseptic and thoroughly cleaned every part of those 14 sites. The doctor had warned of the importance warding off infection, saying, "Infection could travel down the pins and into the bone, and that *would* result in amputation!" The final step was to apply a gummy substance around the pin-site to seal up the wound.

This entire process took my dad 30-45 minutes. Then, he would go to work. At the end of the day, after work, Dad would fix supper and go through the entire cleaning process again before going to bed. The doctor told him he would have to do this for six weeks.

The bones of the lower leg are known as "dumb bones" because they don't heal very quickly. Little tissue is there and very little blood flows around them, so they simply take longer to heal. Because of that, Dad had to do the cleaning procedure for far beyond the predicted six weeks—it took nine long months.

During this time, he truly taught me the key of, COMMIT TO CONSISTENCY. Every morning and evening he was on his knees. He never blew it off, never missed a beat, why? It leads me to the final key.

About 6 months into the healing process, I asked my dad *"Why? Why are you going to all this trouble when the doctor says Mom may not walk again?"* Dad responded without hesitation. *"Because I believe Jesus is going to heal your mom!"* No doubts, no hesitation, simple faith. My dad went on to explain that faith is not just sitting back and expecting God to work some special effects miracle. He showed me that God works His miracles as we work out our faith. Dad was doing everything he could; then he left the rest up to God.

The doctor called it a "medical miracle." My dad says, "It was Jesus!" Today, my mom walks without the aid of a cane or walker or any other devise except the hand of the man who taught me about leadership.

How about you? Are you ready to, discover the leader within? One of the best places to begin is in your own home. Show the world closest to you that you are ready willing and able to give your very best and to do it every day. When the day is done, remember who gave you the opportunity to grow to your leadership potential, and thank God that he has even greater plans for your life then you ever imagined.

EXPECT EXCELLENCE, COMMIT TO CONSISTENCY, and BE FOUNDED IN FAITH. Discover the leader within YOU!

For Eunice

by
BOB LENZ

TEEN
POWER
Thru CHRIST

For Eunice

by
Bob Lenz

Eunice was born to a less than perfect family, in a less than perfect neighborhood. As she grew, she became the victim of her parents' shortcomings. No matter how hard she tried, she was unable to win their affection or approval. Not being perfect herself, she could never live up to her dad's hopes or demands. Longing deeply for his love to fill her emptiness, she tried harder and harder. She felt she was never good enough and entered her teens feeling like a failure.

As a teen, she felt her home was no longer a shelter for her heart. Craving to fit in somewhere, she turned to her friends for acceptance. She was welcomed, and it felt good to be wanted. She felt like she belonged . . . at first. Soon she found out her friends had even higher standards that they expected her to meet: act like this, wear this, be this, listen to this, don't believe that. She tried hard to live up to their expectations, but she failed once again and fell heart-first into the depths of desperation.

Eunice would do anything to numb the pain of hopelessness and build a sense of purpose. She started drinking and soon moved on to other drugs. Then she started noticing the opposite sex. Or should I say, she took note of them noticing her. What started out as just flirting soon turned into an obsession with looks, clothes, and weight. She would do anything to win their attention. Eunice felt that she needed it to survive. She would go to bed with any warm body that would whisper, "I love you," even though she knew it was a lie. In these few moments she could pretend she was valued and wanted—maybe even needed. Morning would bring back the emptiness and destroy her meager attempts to build a life. Her heart was more than broken; it was crushed! She had heard these words too many times; "You're not pretty enough . . . rich enough . . . smart enough . . . popular enough!"

Like a thief in the night, a sense of worthlessness would creep over her and beat her to the ground until she felt she had no choice but to surrender. Eunice was born into an environment that delighted in stripping her of dignity, and she had bought into the lie that she was worthless.

Rest for Her Soul

Eunice was ready to give up, and she felt dead inside. She thought suicide was the only way out of this maze of confusion and pain. At that point, another student from school invited her to a youth group: *"Come along, we would love to have you."* Eunice decided there was nothing to lose. She arrived at the church alone and very skeptical. She was surprised by the way the other teens enjoyed singing "religious" songs. She had never been to church, and this first experience shattered all the concepts of how she had imagined it. This was cool!

The youth director discussed the message of the Bible. He talked about *love without conditions* and *acceptance without performance.* Eunice thought this was too good to be true! Love with no strings attached? This was the kind of love that promised rest for her weary soul. This was the kind of love that brought a ray of hope to her broken heart, a tear to her eye, and goose bumps to her arms!

Could it be true? Could she have new meaning and purpose for her life? Did someone love her *just the way she was?* These questions were spinning in her head. Her heart beat with hope.

Even though most of the kids didn't know her, three people came up and gave her a hug when they introduced themselves. It felt so good to be hugged as a friend, and her heart leapt for joy. Eunice thought, *"Wow! Maybe this is true."* Then they broke into groups to further discuss the love of God portrayed in the Bible. She felt excited about all that had happened that night until she overheard the other kids talking in a small group, *"Did you hear about John and Pete? They were smoking behind the church last week!"*

"That's nothing," said another, *"the deacon's daughter was with . . . and I heard . . . ."*

"Really?" Someone else responded in shock.

Eunice clamed up. Her head dropped in shame. Hope skipped a beat and joy stumbled. She thought, *"if they knew my life story, they would never accept me!"*

They went back to the large group for a final song, but Eunice didn't sing along. The leader closed with a few words and a prayer, but this time Eunice didn't believe what was being said.

After youth group, everyone went out for pizza; everyone except Eunice. No one had invited her, so she left the church the same way she had arrived: alone. Now she felt rejected by God and His people. The weariness in her soul grew even stronger as she walked quietly along the road. With her head bowed and her shoulders slumped, she never saw the car coming at her. She was killed instantly. Eunice left this earth and went into eternity not knowing that anyone was there for her at a time when she could have and should have known the 4-U-NESS of Jesus.

Eunice represents you, me, and every teenager who desperately need to hear the good news of the Gospel.

The 4-U-NESS of God

Jesus demonstrated His 4-U-NESS the night before He died. "And He took bread, gave thanks and broke it, and gave it to them saying, 'This is my body, given [*4-U*]; do this in remembrance of me.' In the same way, after the supper He took the cup, saying, 'This cup is the new covenant in my blood, which is poured out [4-U]'" (Luke 22:19, 20).

God is 4-U, but many people have a hard time believing this. Do you realize the Creator of heaven and earth is head-over-heels in love with you? Yahweh is crazy about you. His love is real. The fact that He is 4-U is true, even when you don't feel it. It is true even when people fail you. God is 4-U even if the church fails you, even if your friends let you down, and even if your own mother and father forsake you. God has promised that He will never leave our side. "I will never abandon you" (Psalm 27:10).

He is different from all others. He is love, perfect love. He is just, and He is pure. He is fair, even when life isn't.

Everyday circumstances attempt to convince us that God doesn't care about us. I wrestle with this concept even as I write this chapter. Just seven days ago, my dad died of a sudden heart attack. I cannot put into words the depth of the pain I am feeling right now because only 13 months ago I lost my mom to cancer, and she was only 63.

I share my pain with you, so that when life's circumstances makes you want to scream out "God doesn't care about me!"—Stop! Take another look at the promise of communion. Then take comfort and remember this; God is 4-U!

If God is 4-U, who can be against you? (Romans 8:31)

Nothing can separate you from the love of God—not trouble or hardship, persecution or poverty, danger; not even death itself can separate us from the love of God! (Romans 8:38, 39) That means, not even the mistakes you've made or the sins you've committed thus far in your life can come between you and God's love for you.

I want you to know and believe . . .

- Jesus was born 4-U (Luke 2:7).
- Jesus lived a sinless life 4-U (2 Corinthians 5:21).
- Jesus prayed to His Father 4-U (Luke 22:32).
- Jesus was whipped, beaten and suffered 4-U (I Peter 2:21).
- Jesus took nails in His hands and feet 4-U (John 20:25–27).
- Jesus died on the cross 4-U (Mark 15:39).
- Jesus rose from the dead 4-U (Acts 2:24).
- Jesus offers forgiveness 4-U (Matthew 26:28).
- Jesus has a heart of love 4-U (John 13:34).
- Jesus' grace is sufficient 4-U (2 Corinthians 12:9).
- God has a plan 4-U (Jeremiah 29:11).
- God has a purpose 4-U (Exodus 9:16).
- Jesus is in heaven building a mansion 4-U (John 14:2).

- Jesus is coming back 4-U (John 14:3).
- Jesus cares so much 4-U (1 Peter 5:7).
- Jesus has won eternal life 4-U (John 6:40, 54).

Chapter

9

Sex and Love – God's Way!

by
ELLEN MARIE

TEEN POWER
Thru CHRIST

Sex and Love – God's Way!

by
ELLEN MARIE

Hang on for a ride. This chapter is for those who dare to want true love, not the kind of superficial lust portrayed in one episode of a sitcom. It contains information to help you better understand the dynamics of romance, and why the glamour of casual sex will never produce lasting true love.

What Does God Say About Sex?

"For this cause a man shall leave his father and mother, and shall cleave to his wife; and the two shall become one flesh."
Ephesians 5:31

God has laid out a map for fulfillment, not just directions to a temporary destination for momentary pleasure. Relationships, marriage and sex are God's ideas. God has given us our sexuality as a gift.

Okay, so God says sex is good, but the Bible also says: *"It is God's will that you should be sanctified: that you should avoid sexual immorality, that each of you should learn to control your body. For God did not call us to be impure, but to live a holy life"* (1 Thessalonians 4:3–7).

Some people wrongfully assume if something is good, more must be better.

> After I gave a chastity speech at a Christian school, a few junior guys approached me with questions. *"Ellen, didn't God create sex?"*

> *"Of course,"* I immediately answered.

> *"Well, if God created sex, and it feels good, why shouldn't we just have sex with as many people as possible? God wants us to be happy, doesn't He?"* they reasoned.

What an interesting argument. They were right—God created sex. They were right again—God wants people to be happy. What they missed, however, is that God wants us fulfilled in the long run more than He wants us to have instant gratification.

Imagine telling your parents that you don't think getting up for school is fun anymore, that you would be much happier if you could just sleep all day. In this scenario, your parents would say your happiness is what matters most. So, if you want to skip school, it's okay with them. Would that be a wise decision? No. Doing things the easy way is not always the best way, and this holds true in the area of sexuality as well. God will always be more concerned with you obtaining lasting love rather than superficial relationships.

The Building Blocks of Love

Make a list of the qualities you desire in a dating relationship. (Yes, you can write in a book as long as it is *your* book.)

1.

2.

3.

4.

Today's Date: _____

Most people's list includes characteristics like trust, respect, physical attraction, good communication, friendship, commitment and love. Understandably, these qualities are the building blocks of a solid relationship. On the other hand, impatient people start with a sexual relationship and mistakenly try to build a solid relationship from there. That approach usually doesn't create a firm foundation to develop into true and lasting love.

Good Communication

Good communication includes listening to your date, asking questions, sharing your opinions, and honestly discussing problems or differences. Developing communication takes practice and effort.

Almost everyone agrees that communication is an important part of any relationship, especially a healthy dating relationship. The God-given pleasure of sex can be a temporary replacement for working at communication.

Last year, after a school assembly I presented on sexual abstinence, a male student told me his story. For a year he and his girlfriend would have sex to "solve" their problems. They fought, ignored the problems, and had sex, which temporarily made them feel close, bonded. This offered a quick fix, but their problems kept getting bigger. Not surprisingly, they eventually broke up.

Unfortunately, some people get married for the joys of sex only to later realize that they didn't know how to communicate or—even worse—that they hardly knew each other. To be sure you really know the person you are dating and have developed communication and friendship, wait until marriage for a sexual relationship.

Sex helps bond two people together. This is good for a marriage. When sex is involved in a dating relationship, however, it makes breaking up even more painful.

A guy recently told me,
"Since most teen relationships don't last, why make it harder on yourself to move on by having sex?"

Trust and Respect

Most people agree trust is critical for a long lasting, fulfilling relationship. How is trust developed? Trust is developed over time and is based on a person's current and past behavior.

A high school female once told me,
*"If you have sex, guys will call you a lot more often.
But you never really know if they like you
or just the sex."*

When a couple enjoys the pleasures of sex without a marital commitment, it is less clear whether they are staying in the relationship because they like the person or the pleasures of sex. We all want relationships in which we are convinced the other person won't cheat and won't just use us. But when a person through his or her actions depicts sex as no big deal, it is more difficult to trust him or her.

What if your date reveals through actions that he or she will have sex without any commitment? How can you be sure that he or she will not repeat this behavior with someone else while still dating you? Furthermore, what do your actions reveal about *your* attitudes on sex and commitment?

Show the person you are dating that you can control your sex drive. Reveal through your actions that you are in the relationship, not to fulfill your own sexual desires but to develop a relationship. Just think how exciting and fulfilling it will be if you develop a solid relationship, commit to one another in marriage, and in that secure relationship express your love sexually.

A 25-year-old man I know admitted,
"I want a women's heart. If I get the sexual relationship first, I lose respect. There is no reason to pursue any longer. For the right girl, I would wait."

In his book, *Mars and Venus on a Date*, Dr. John Gray shows appreciation for this point of view when he writes about how women think differently than men. For instance, he explains that a woman mistakenly assumes that if she is eager to please a man, he will become more interested in her. Dr. Gray then points out that the opposite is true, that a man quickly pleased by a woman is typically less likely to pursue her. Why? According to him, a man is most fulfilled through being successful at fulfilling a woman. Dr. Gray was not only referring to the sexual relationship. In other words, no matter what a guy receives, he feels better when he believes that he actively pursued and achieved it. Men like feeling successful.

Friendship and Love

Several years ago, I was very much in love with a man and he with me. We dated and were best friends. One day he told me in a soft voice how much he loved me, and he thanked me for choosing to abstain from sex in our relationship.

Though he had been sexually active in other relationships, he eventually realized that sex confused him. He was never sure whether he liked the girl or just the physical intimacy. Because of our abstinence, he said that he fell in love with me for "all the right reasons." Hearing that felt so good!

It is normal to occasionally be confused and to have questions in dating relationships. However, a sexual relationship before marriage can lead a person into thinking the relationship is solid, when in reality it is only based upon lust.

In his book, *Finding the Love of Your Life*, Neil Clark Warren, Ph.D. writes, *"Once you have become sexually involved with a potential mate, your ability to think clearly and objectively becomes impossible."* So, couples that have premarital sex rob themselves of their own ability to look clearly at their relationship and to make the best decision about who and who not to marry. Give yourself time to get to know the person you date—without sexual confusion. Abstinence gives you freedom to not be confused.

Fresh Starts

You may be reading this chapter thinking, *"Hey, this makes some sense."* On the other hand, you may think it is too late for you.

A high school girl once told me,
"It is too late for me. I'm living with my boyfriend. I've had an abortion. How can I even look at God now?"

But starting over is what Christianity is all about. If you think it is too late to start over, if you think Jesus will not forgive you, then everything Jesus did on the cross—dying a painful death—was all for nothing. Would you go to Jesus and tell Him His dying on the cross just wasn't enough for you? The Bible is filled with verses to encourage you to ask

God for forgiveness. Consider Jeremiah 3:11: *"I will frown on you no longer, for I am merciful, declares the Lord: I will not be angry forever, only acknowledge your guilt . . ."*

If you have not been respecting the people you date, you can start over. Go to God today. Tell Him from your heart how you feel. Then, ask for forgiveness and the strength to change.

Though God can and will forgive, many people cannot accept God's forgiveness or forgive themselves. Instead, they keep bringing up past mistakes and dwelling on them. What does God say about how *He* feels about our sins once we ask forgiveness? *"Though your sins are as scarlet, they will be as white as snow"* (Isaiah 1:18). So, confess your mistakes, ask for forgiveness, and let it go. You should be aware, however, that although God will forgive you, your choices may still have physical and emotional consequences.

Single With a Purpose

One of the most difficult areas for most people to wait upon God is with their love lives. We have it all planned out. We want to be married to our prince or princess by age 21, live in the perfect house, and work at the ideal job. We want to spend our weekends shopping, sitting by the pool, or working on our motorcycles.

Many people do not see God's perfect timing and plan for their lives in the area of relationships. You may have found the best person for you. Others have not. I meet plenty of teens who are heartsick because they have not met the right person. Do you know for sure that the best person for you is in your school? Is there a possibility that you need to grow spiritually and learn more about yourself before you join with another person for life?

Oh, how painful it can be to wait upon God! Yet, giving God time to help you grow closer to Him is a good thing. Psalm 37:4 states, *"Delight yourself in the Lord, and He will give you the desires of your heart."* Ask God to prepare you for your future mate. Start praying today for your future mate. Yet, remember to focus first on God.

If you get married sooner, later or never, remember that the years of being single can be used very productively. You can travel, go on a mission trip, complete college, pursue a career, develop your talents and—most importantly—grow in your faith. As you mature in each area, you will be more prepared to choose a spouse similar to you, someone who shares your interests and faith.

Are you willing to develop yourself during your single years and in this way have more to offer your future spouse? Are you willing to use your single years for God? Consider these encouraging words from Jeremiah 1:7: *"But the Lord said to me: Do not say, "I am a youth," because everywhere you go I shall send you."*

You were born for a reason! Ask God to use your single years, no matter how long or short they may be. To this end, I recommend reading *When God Writes Your Love Story* by Eric and Leslie Ludy. Also, keep in mind that women and men see romantic relationships from different perspectives. Here are some insights:

For Women Only

Over the years, single men have shared thoughts with me that you deserve to know. For instance, many women feel the quickest way to earn a guy's love is through sex, but a *mature* man is looking for a woman to respect. He is searching for someone "worth waiting for," someone who respects herself.

> A girl from my high school once told me,
> *"If you give a guy sex, he will stay with you."*

It didn't work for her, and it doesn't work for most girls. Women who use sex to lure a man are selling themselves short. If a woman tries to convince a man to continue dating her just because she is good in bed, it only tells him that her body is all she has to offer. If a woman indicates that her body is all she has to offer, a man will agree and treat her the same way that she believes she should be treated. Respect your body.

Ladies, your personality, talents, virtue, attractiveness, and charm are what make a man want to continue dating you. Let a man get to know *you*, so he can determine what makes you unique and special. In turn, admire your date and build him up with true, positive comments. Let him know how you appreciate the little things he does for you, and that you respect him for who he is.

For Men Only

Guys, even if a girl does not want to date you, she is usually flattered that you had the guts to ask her out. When you do go on a date, it is much better to err on the side of chivalry. Although a few women may not show appreciation when you act like gentlemen, most love it when men hold the door open for them, treat them like ladies, and give them genuine compliments. Give it a try.

However, *please* don't lie and tell a girl you love her or give her compliments in hopes that she will give you more physically. You may cause her to not trust other guys. And hey, some day, you may be the "other guy" who isn't being trusted through no fault of your own.

Deep down, we really want men to respect and protect us as women. Think of how you want someone to treat your sister or mother, then treat the women you date that way. Help us establish a good reputation by not using us for your own pleasure, even if on the surface some women don't appear to care. If you treat us with respect, we may better determine our love for you. Then, we will both live out the fulfilling plan of love God has designed for His children.

For Women and Men

Remember to treat each person you date with respect, even if you determine he or she is not the person for you. If you do not marry him or her, someone else probably will. So, don't degrade your date's self-esteem. Finally, ask God to guide your relationships and your future—starting today.

Chapter

10

Rock the Party!

by
BOBBY PETROCELLI

TEEN
POWER
Thru CHRIST

Rock the Party!

by
BOBBY PETROCELLI

During the summer of 2000, two new hard-core rock bands exploded onto the music scene and were featured frequently on MTV's "Total Request Live" show. The bands are similar in their sound, style and excitement, but their similarity ends there. When I first saw Papa Roach's song "The Last Resort" played, I loved the music but found myself troubled by the message. Their words echoed desperation, anger, and pain with lyrics screaming *"suffocation/ no breathing/ my life is in pieces/ this is my last resort/ I am losing my sight/ losing my mind/I wish somebody would tell me I am fine."* It has been said that people perish without hope for the future. Certainly Papa Roach's song is without hope.

On the other hand, P.O.D. (Payable on Death) is a band with a similar sound but a decisively different message. Their song, "Rock the Party" received rave reviews on MTV. After they were interviewed on Total Request Live, Host Carson Daly said, *"What P.O.D. said was the best thing ever said on this stage, they said, 'We have found some-thing great in this world and want to share it'."* P.O.D. was talking about their faith in God and how they share it through their music. They personify the reality that ministry strategy is always subject to change. That is, **the MESSAGE is sacred, but the METHOD isn't!**

P.O.D.'s "Rock the Party" music video portrays the band on a bus—light illuminating from every opening—traveling to the greatest party of all time. Along the way, they pick up people of all colors, shapes, sizes, and fashion styles to take them to this party. Their anthem, *"We came here to Rock this jam! to spread His love is the master plan!"* The final video scene depicts the crowd partying in front of a mural that is a modern day depiction of Jesus on the Cross. This video ROCKS! This modern rock band is proud to proclaim the greatest love of all—the love of Jesus Christ! It is as if they are saying to the bands like Papa Roach, *"You are fine because God loves you, not because you are somebody. The Lord wants to make you somebody!"*

Society's version of love says *you have to measure up.* God's love has no conditions! His love is both constant *and* consistent! God's unconditional love is not based on what we do or we don't do; for example, *He would love us more if . . . He loves me less because . . .* No, God's love is not performance driven! Romans 8:38, 39 teaches that **nothing** on this earth can ever separate us from God's love. **Nothing** we could ever do would keep us from the grasp of Jesus' outstretched arms. He loves us like we are the only one on this earth to love. He loves those who may be considered unlovable or unlivable. He is not concerned with where you have been or where you are; He is tender to where you are going.

From This Moment On

To gain acceptance as a Cadet in the United States Air Force Academy in Colorado Springs, a student must meet rigorous academic, athletic, and character standards. The moment that student is enrolled as an official Air Force Academy Cadet, however, his or her past successes and failures are no longer relevant. All that matters to the Air Force is what the person does from that point on.

What will you do from this point on? You can continue to dwell on your past good or bad or you can begin anew in the arms of the Lord. Personally, I have never met anyone who regrets turning his or her life over to God. I've never heard anyone say, *"You know, I wish I never invited Jesus Christ into my heart."* The awesome truth is that Christ's hand always reaches out to those who reach to Him. So why would you not want to come rock at the greatest party of all?

A True Servant of the Lord

Jessica was a beautiful 17-year old high school senior. Two days before prom, she rushed home excitedly to show her mother her new haircut. This wasn't just any haircut—she had gotten them all cut, right down to the scalp. Jessica had shaved her head completely bald! Understandably, her mother freaked out. *"Jessica, I can't believe you shaved off your beautiful, red curly hair right before your senior prom! What were you thinking? Look at you now—you were the Homecoming Queen. There is no way, absolutely, no way—you will ever be named Prom Queen; not looking like that!*

You ought to be ashamed! Go to your room! I can't stand looking at you! Wait 'til your father hears about this!"

Jessica ran to her room crying hysterically. *"Ma, you don't understand. You just don't understand!"*

Two long hours passed before her mother came to Jessica's closed bedroom door where she could her Jessica sobbing. *"Jessica, let me in. I want to talk to you."*

After several seconds of awkward anticipation, Jessica reluctantly opened the door and let her mother in. With tears still streaming down her face, Jessica sat on the edge of her bed with her eyes fixated on the carpet patterns below. The ensuing fifteen seconds of silence seemed like an eternity as her mother paced hurriedly back and forth across the floor. Her jaw jutted out in repressed anger as she fumed at Jessica. *"What in the w—what in the w—!"* Finally, after two unsuccessful attempts to voice her disbelief, she was able to vocalize her mounting frustration. *"What in the world possessed you to do this? What were you thinking? Who told you to do this? Who was it? One of your friends? It was one of your friends, wasn't it? It had to be. You wouldn't do this kind of thing on your own. That's not like you,"* she continued. *"What kind of friend would have so much influence over you—to make you so rebellious to do something like this? I just don't understand it. I really don't."*

Jessica hesitated for a moment, then tearfully lifted her head and in a strained voice, began to reply. *"You never gave me a chance to explain. As soon as I walked in the door you jumped all over me, and I didn't even have a chance to tell you why I did it. It was Mary, Mom. Mary made me do it."*

Her mom snapped back, *"Well, you just give me Mary's phone number right now—I want to speak to her mother and give her a piece of my mind and tell her what kind of daughter has—to be such a negative influence on you! What kind of girl is this Mary? What's her number? I'm calling her right now, this instant! I have never seen something so crazy in my entire life."*

It was now Jessica's turn to speak. *"Mom, Mary dropped out of school seven weeks ago. During that time, nobody knew what happened to her, and nobody has been allowed to see her. You see, Mom, she has cancer and has been receiving chemotherapy treatments."* Tears began once again to well in her eyes. *"Her seven weeks of treatments ended yesterday, and when she finally returned to school today, after all that time—she was bald, I mean completely bald. No hair on her head at all! No eyebrows, no nothing—not even hair on her arms. She had to wear a red bandanna like a babushka to cover her bald head—but people still made fun of her. The boys were especially cruel, calling her 'cueball, chrome dome, bald eagle,' things like that. My heart broke for her. I decided right then and there that I didn't care how I looked in my prom pictures. I wanted Mary to know that she would never have to walk through the halls of our school alone. If people were going to make fun of her, they would have to make fun of me, too. I decided that I would be there for her and I* *would be there **with** her. I wanted her to also know that somebody loved her—and that somebody would be me."*

When I share Jessica's story in school assemblies or college programs, I tell the students, *"If I went to Jessica's school, I would be the first guy crawling after her, groveling at her feet, and begging her to be my girlfriend. She's exactly the type of girl I would want to be with because she knows what it means to give her life for a friend."* **Jessica understands one of the most important principles in life: the further she gets from herself and the further she gets from her own needs, the closer she gets to the heart of God!**

Do you possess the courage of Jessica? Would you allow yourself to be humiliated if it meant that you would be doing something great for somebody else? Are you willing to pay that stiff of a price? Society tells us to look out only for ourselves. *It's all about me. Me, me, me, me, me—I'm all that!* God tells us that in order to receive the truly great rewards, we first have to be willing to give. *"Give and it shall be given unto you!"* Those who are servants *first* are greatest in God's kingdom and they exemplify the portrayal of faith and strength. Pray for the courage of Jessica and ask God for opportunities to practice your Christian servanthood.

Get Out of YOUR Comfort Zone— Get Into GOD's Zone!

Never think that you can't be a servant of the Lord because you feel you are lacking time, money, or talent. Have faith in God and faith in yourself! Faith breeds love and promise—while fear breeds doubt, guilt, and condemnation. God is not concerned with what you have; He is only concerned with what you *do* with what you have! **Don't get trapped in thinking, "I don't have anything to give"—give what you** *do* **have!** If you are going to err, err on the side of over-giving! Be generous to a fault. You can never give enough of yourself or your resources in the service of the Lord.

Feel God's calling of you and your talents to grab the attention of your entire family, all of your friends, and your whole school by doing great things to impact other lives. What's holding you back? You may not be the first person God has called to make a difference in your school, or in your family, or among your friends, but you *could* be the first to obey His call! The only thing that counts for anything in life is what you do for God—by serving Him and serving others! The motto of the Hard-Rock Cafe is, "Serve one; Serve all!" As a Christian, take on that motto, but add to it, **"LOVE ONE; LOVE ALL!"**

You Have Been Chosen!

Sometimes we get lulled into thinking that we have to be or act—a certain way for God to use us. This isn't true at all. More than anything, God wants people to be available. That's all He asks us to be—available! He doesn't call the perfect; He perfects us and *then* develops our gifts. He doesn't call the anointed or the equipped; He anoints and equips those whom He calls.

Moses was a chronic stutterer and didn't think God would use him. God shaped Moses and used him to lead the Israelites out of Egypt and out of bondage. Peter spent three years with Jesus, and then betrayed Him. Nonetheless, Christ told Peter, *"On you, I will build my church"* (Matthew 16:18). Walt Disney was fired from his first job for lack of imagination, but I don't have to tell you what happened to him or his ideas! You, too, have been chosen to serve. Have you answered the call?

Needs vs. Wants: The Land of Confusion

Jimmy returned home from a wonderful week at church camp, just in time to go on his weekly summer fishing trip with his Grandpa. As they drove down the road to their favorite fishing hole, Jimmy described how wonderful the camp was. He told Gramps, *"I learned so much about wanting to be used by God. I want to be a voice in the wilderness. I want to make a difference."* His grandfather smiled. When they reached the fishing hole, Grandpa and Jimmy set up on their favorite rock. As Jimmy began to bait his hook, Gramps grabbed Jimmy by the back of the neck and pushed his head underwater. Ten . . . twenty . . . thirty seconds passed. Jimmy struggled to break free, desperately trying to come up for air. Finally, after almost a minute, Grandpa finally released him. Jimmy, now panicked, gasped for air and screamed at his Grandfather, *"Are you crazy, Grandpa? What are you doing? Are you trying to kill me? Why did you do that?"* Grandpa replied, *"Whenever you desire God to work in your life like you desired for that breath of air, then and only then, can God work within your life in such an awesome way."*

Our salvation is a gift; godliness is a pursuit! God is very concerned with what we *need* but not always concerned with what we *want*. Choices based on pleasure, rather than discipline and experience will always lead to failure! In wanting be used by God, you have to be willing to be prepared by Him. If you dance with the devil, he never changes, but he changes you.

The paradox of life is spelled out in God's word. Matthew 16:25 tells us that the only way we gain in this world is by first losing our selves by exchanging our self-centered motives for the motivation and life of God. Matthew 23:12 states that the only way to be built up in this world is to first humble ourselves. John 12:24 proclaims that the only way to truly live is to first die to our own desires and then take on God's desires.

The message is clear—people who wait for God to come *for* them miss out because God wants to first come *to* them. Come to God in heart, mind, and service. *Rock on with the greatest party of all; the Party of the Lord!*

Chapter

11

Three Marks of Christianity

by
<u>TERRY PRISK</u>

TEEN POWER
Thru CHRIST

Three Marks of Christianity

by

TERRY PRISK

Marks. Distinctives. Uniquenesses. Every person on this planet has his or her own version of these—but what makes a Christian different? What distinguishing marks does a Christian carry? What is it about you, as a Christian, that makes you stand out from everyone else? Let's explore what it means for you, as a Christian, to carry special marks on your life showing that you belong to Christ.

I love to travel, and my speaking schedule has allowed me to visit many different places and meet many interesting people. I am always struck by the amazing uniqueness of people. No two are alike—and some are *really* different. Consider just people's hairstyles. Some go for short, long, or even various shades of purple. In my case, I go for the wet look—as in, when I sweat during a talk, I create my own personal water slide. It's a distinctive that God gave me. A bald head.

Consider the differences in people's body types. I have had the privilege on several occasions to speak to professional sports teams. The first time that I spoke for the Detroit Tigers, I met their catcher. This guy had an unbelievable upper body! Definitely very distinctive from mine! I distinctly remember him and many of the other athletes I've met. Why? There was something unique about their body types (and I was impressed!).

On another occasion, I met a very unique person I won't easily forget—but for other reasons. I was at an amusement park and thought that I recognized a girl. I went up to her, grabbed her arm, and said, "Hey, how are you?" When she turned around and looked at me, I realized that I did not know her. I also realized that she had a boyfriend—a very *big* boyfriend, a very *big, unhappy* boyfriend. He had a patch over one eye, lots of tattoos, and looked like he had just hopped off a large motorcycle. He didn't like that I had touched his lady, and he began to come after me. Being an individual who resists pain, I began to run toward a restroom and jumped into a stall. I hopped up on the toilet, praying, "Please, please...." (I wonder how this sounded to the guy next to me?). Fortunately, the big guy ran right on through the restroom and out the other door. If I saw that guy today, I would run again. I remember what he looked like. He had certain distinctive marks that I will never forget.

Let me give you another example. Several years ago, I was at a camp in Wisconsin doing some water-skiing. I was attempting to slalom ski from a dock start. I had just maneuvered the slack in the rope and was prepared to jump off the dock when I heard a voice behind me. It was a young lady who wanted to ski double! What made this unique was that she had only one leg. Obviously she could slalom! She took her artificial leg off and set it on the dock. I'll never forget this girl. She was certainly unique!

What do these three people have in common? Why will I never forget them? All of these people had a certain characteristic that was readily identifiable. In the same way, I believe Christians should have certain distinctives, or marks. From James 1:26-27, I see three distinctive marks that should be in every Christian's life:

> *"If anyone considers himself religious and yet does not keep a tight reign on his tongue, he deceives himself and his religion is worthless. Religion that God our Father accepts as pure and faultless is this: to look after orphans and widows in their distress and to keep oneself from being polluted by the world."*

The three distinctives described in these verses will mark you as a Christian, letting the people around you see that you know and belong to Christ. Let's explore these one at a time.

Speaking Well

The first mark that others should notice about you as a Christian is your *controlled tongue*. James calls this knowing how to "keep a tight rein" on what spills out of your mouth. In other words, your speech should be thoughtful and careful.

I have great respect for a particular friend of mine. When he walks into a room, he attracts attention. Why? He is very distinguished in his appearance. But even more than that, something about his behavior is unique. It took me awhile to catch on to what makes him so different from everyone else. Whenever he is in a conversation, he pauses before he responds. At first, I thought he just didn't know what to say. Now I see that, during those pauses, he is thinking through his choice of words. Because of that, what he has to say always has great wisdom. James 1:19 says, "Be quick to listen, slow to speak." For many people, it is the other way around—they speak way too often, too soon, and without much thought. They are not controlling their tongues.

So how should a Christian talk? Ephesians 4:29 offers excellent advice: "Do not let any unwholesome talk come out of your mouths, but only what is helpful for building others up according to their needs, that it may benefit those who listen." Is your talk characteristically wholesome or unwholesome? Do you show respect to adults? Do you speak positively to your parents? Do you keep your mouth shut when others begin to gossip? Do you stop before you speak and ask, "Jesus, what would you have me say?" Do your words build people up or tear them down?

What a difference it would make if we, as Christians, controlled our mouths! What a distinctive mark that should be! I remember being in my high school biology class and, because we had a substitute teacher, I was sending notes to the beautiful girl sitting next to me. I decided that because the substitute looked wimpy and because I was an athlete and class officer, I could get away with it. The substitute suddenly caught me, saying, "Terry Prisk, what are you doing?"

I looked up. "We're playing a game," I said calmly.

He responded, "Bring that game to me."

My oh-so-cool response was, "If you want it, you come and get it."

Obviously, my tongue was not in control!

Years later, when I became the Director of Student Ministries at a church, I looked out in the sanctuary and saw that man from my past—that substitute teacher. I was in a dilemma. After all those years, I had to make this right. I walked up to him and said, "I owe you an apology. My tongue was out of control in a biology class many years ago. It wasn't right. Will you forgive me?" And he did.

Is your tongue under control? Is there somebody you need to approach to ask for forgiveness because you said something you shouldn't have said? The first distinctive mark of a Christian is that you are careful with your words—you have a controlled tongue.

Reaching Out

The second mark that others should notice about you as a Christian is that you are *helping the helpless and reaching out to those in need.* James continued, "Religion that God our Father accepts as pure and faultless is this: to look after orphans and widows in their distress."

After a retreat a young man named Chris approached me. He said, "Terry, on the retreat, I really feel that God spoke to me. I need to do something special for someone. I'm going to a convalescent home near my home and visit someone who doesn't have many visitors or family." I thought that was commendable and encouraged him.

The following week, Chris came up to me saying that he needed to talk about a problem. I immediately thought that he had not followed through on his commitment to go to the convalescent center and was feeling guilty about it. But I was wrong. Chris said, "I visited the convalescent home and approached an aide. She told me about an elderly man who never had any visitors." When Chris visited the man's room, he ran into a problem. The old man wanted to play chess, and Chris didn't know how. *That* was a problem! So we got Chris some help and he learned to play chess. Then, faithfully once a week, Chris played chess with an older gentleman no one else cared about. That's reaching out to those in need. That's caring.

How can you help the helpless and reach out to those in need? You don't have to look too far. When was the last time that you visited your grandpa and grandma and told them how much you love them? How about mowing a lawn for a widow and expecting no money in return? How about raking the leaves or doing errands for a disabled person? This is the kind of religion that our God and Father accepts as pure and faultless. This is what the world needs—students who will make a difference and respond like Jesus would respond. There are people in your family, neighborhood, and community who need a special touch. They need *your* touch.

During the Christmas season, I have been involved in a project called, "Operation Scrooge." It stands for Students' Christmas Rush for Oodles and Oodles of Goodies, Etc. In cooperation with an organization like the Salvation Army, this project involves collecting canned goods to provide food for needy families for the Christmas season and months thereafter. One year, I remember going out with the students on a very cold evening. At one house, a woman pulled up in her station wagon just as we were knocking at her door. She had obviously just gone shopping. She had at least fifteen bags of groceries in her vehicle. I told her what we were doing and that we'd like some canned goods for needy people. She said, "I'm sorry, we have nothing to give." It took everything in me not to throw her into a snow bank. But knowing that such an act would not be a Christ-like example, I refrained (but I have to tell you, I considered doing it and then asking for forgiveness!).

Two or three doors down the street, a smiling elderly woman greeted us and invited us in for hot chocolate. We passed on her invitation, but told her about our project. She brought us inside and directed us to her pantry. She didn't say, "Take two or three cans." She said, "Take everything." We responded that we couldn't take everything from her, for then she would have nothing. She said, "Sure you can. God will provide for me. The people for whom you are collecting food need these far more than I do." This woman was a giver.

Later, we went to the Salvation Army with over 400 cans. As we dropped them off, we noticed that there were only 23 other cans of food already in the pantry. A new believer named Debbie, who was with us, asked the commander what would have happened if we had not brought the 400 cans. He simply replied, "Well, we would not have had food to give."

Debbie, this young new believer, said, "Wait a second. We have to be able to get more. I am going to get my friends to go and get additional cans." She asked the commander if he could meet her at 11:00 p.m. on the next Friday night. She then mobilized a group of her friends who were attending a party that night. At 11:00 p.m., as the commander and I waited in the parking lot, several vehicles pulled up with hundreds of cans. This new believer had exhibited one of the distinctive marks of Christianity—helping others.

You know how people can see that you have been touched by God? When you are willing to reach out to help the helpless. When you go beyond your comfort zone. When you help those who may never be able to reciprocate. That's religion that God our Father accepts as pure and faultless. Do you need to become aware of the needs that surround you? Do you need to help others? The second distinctive mark of a Christian is that you have a helping spirit.

Living Right

The third mark that others should notice about you as a Christian is that you *live a holy life*. James wrote that believers should not be "polluted by the world." Christians should not be chameleons! You are called to live a holy life in an unholy world. This does not mean you have to be perfect. To be "holy" means to be "set apart." It means realizing that you have a high calling, you have the Holy Spirit within you, and you have the deep desire to be like Christ.

Once when I was at the beach on a youth event, a young man named Mark made an impact on me. Mark was a good-looking guy. I noticed that while we were catching some rays, Mark always laid on his stomach. Then, all of a sudden later that afternoon, Mark was gone. When we all headed to the bus to go home, Mark was already on the bus. I asked him, "Mark, where were you?"

He answered, "I just headed off by myself."

"Mark, that's not like you," I said, surprised. "You enjoy a good time. Everybody likes to be around you. So why did you take off?"

His reply surprised me even more. "Terry," he said quietly, "My mind was going nuts out there on that beach. Seeing all those girls and the way they were dressed. I had to get away from it. If I am really going to be a follower of Christ, then I have to keep my mind pure." Believers need to keep their thoughts unpolluted. In order to do that, Mark got out of the tempting situation.

Do you keep yourself out of compromising situations? Is your music pure? Are you careful about which movies and videos you watch? God wants you to live an unpolluted life. The third distinctive mark of a Christian is that you are seeking to live a holy life through the power of Christ working in you.

Being Marked

You, as a Christian, should have these three distinctive marks in your life:

1. A controlled tongue.
2. A helping spirit.
3. A holy (unpolluted) life.

Do you have these three marks? Are you an unforgettable Christian? Will people remember you because of these distinctive marks? I trust that the people you touch every day will never forget you because you have these three marks of Christianity in your life.

Get Under the Umbrella

by
<u>LORI SALIERNO</u>

TEEN POWER
Thru CHRIST

Get Under the Umbrella

by

Lori Salierno

Principles were created by God to govern human life and provide us with many blessings. Those who live a principle-centered life will excel. On the other hand, those who chose to ignore God's principles ultimately experience pain and failure. God's principles are universal in that they are truths that apply to all people, at all times, and in all places. They transcend time and culture. These principles are like umbrellas; if you bring your life under the umbrella, it will provide protection for you. If, however, you take your life out from underneath the protection of the umbrella, you will lose the safety and shelter provided by its principles.

The Principle of Respect

A few years ago I went to Calcutta, India to work in homes started by Mother Teresa. One of the homes we visited was for mentally challenged kids. As we entered, a seven year old girl with crippled legs, deformed arms, bulging belly, crossed eyes, and balding head came up to me and grabbed onto my leg, crying *"Auntie, Auntie, Auntie."* As

I did my work, the little girl continued to hang on to my leg crying *"Auntie, Auntie."* About 11/2 hours later I wanted to fling her off of my leg because she was frustrating me. (You could say that I had some growing to do.)

One of the sisters must have read my face because she said to me, *"Do you want to know why this little one calls you Auntie?"* The sister continued, *"When she was about three years old, her mother left her in the gutter to die. A woman from your country with light hair and fair skin found her in the gutter and took her home to her guesthouse. This woman bathed her, fed her, clothed her, and told her Bible stories. She told the little girl that she was important and valuable to God. The little girl called this woman Auntie. When the woman's visa ran out, she brought the little girl to this home for us to care for her. When she saw you come in with your light hair and fair skin she thought her Auntie had come back to get her. Lori, you represent to her the person and the first time anyone ever cared for her and respected her as a human being."* I hugged the little girl and realized that another person from our country had kept this little girl from becoming a statistic. That particular lady loved this little girl and valued her enough to raise her quality of life.

Even though I never met the mysterious woman with light hair and fair skin, she taught me the true meaning of respect—to value life, all life. Respect is living the Golden Rule: to *"do unto others as you would have them do unto you"* (Matthew 7:12). Every time you treat someone with respect, you actually raise that person's quality of life. We may not respect the things that some people do, but we need to treat everyone with respect just the same.

Clean Lessons from Dirty Work

My first two years in college, I earned money by cleaning the dormitory bathrooms. This was not the greatest job in the world, but it provided the money I needed for school. In my third year of college I got a job as a receptionist in a courthouse. The second day of that job, a young man came in pushing a cart loaded with Windex, cleansers, paper towels, and brushes. He looked as though he was about 18-years-old, and his muscles were cut and tight. I noticed that his shoulders were slumped as he went in to clean the small bathroom in our office. As he was leaving I said, *"Hi sir, my name is Lori, what is yours?"* As he walked out the door he mumbled, *"Dexter."* Two days later he came in again, shoulders slumped, dragging his feet, no expression on his face, pushing the cart to go clean our bathroom. It was obvious that he lacked self-respect. As he was leaving our office, I said, *"Dexter, can I tell you something about yourself? You don't like your job!"*

"No kidding; I clean toilets for a living," he responded.

"Well the next time, after you finish," I said, *"I am going to grade your toilet. I had to clean toilets for two years to earn money to go to school, and I am the best toilet cleaner there is!"*

He looked at me and said, *"You're weird."*

The next week he came in and walked up to my desk. Looking around to make sure the secretaries would not hear him, he said, "*You really gonna grade my toilet today?*"

"*Yep!*" I replied.

After 15 minutes of cleaning the tiny bathroom, Dexter was ready for me to evaluate his work. I went in the bathroom, lifted the lid of the toilet, and was very un-impressed by the results. "*Dexter, the best grade I can give you is a 'C'.*"

He was shocked and said, "*I spent 15 minutes in there clean-ing when I usually spend 5-8 minutes. I deserve a better grade.*"

"*You will get a better grade when you do better work,*" I answered.

Two days later he came in, his shoulders were higher, and he had a smile on his face, ready to get an A. He had spent 25 minutes cleaning the bathroom this time. I went in and it looked much better, but I noticed that he had left something behind. I said, "*What's this? You left a micro-scopic piece of toilet tissue. I can only give you a B.*"

"*I deserve an A,*" said Dexter.

"*You will get an A when you do A work. Remember, I am the expert toilet cleaner,*" I said.

Dexter must have thought that I was the weirdest woman he had ever met. The next week as I was answering phones, I looked up and there was a toilet brush in my face. This time, with a big grin, Dexter cleaned for 45 minutes. Finally, he came out and said, "*Come check this out!*" I went in the bathroom and it was sparkling clean. I could have eaten my lunch on the floor of that bathroom.

"*Dexter, you get an A+!*"

"*YAHOO!*" he exclaimed with genuine excitement. Dexter then invited me into the break room to meet his friends who he had told about the toilet grading. One of the guys cleaned windows and asked me to grade his windows. Another guy trimmed hedges and wanted me to grade his work as well. I realized that these guys wanted to be valued and respected, and no one had ever shown them that kind of respect. Instead, they had been treated like robots.

I told each of worker that he was very important to the operation of the courthouse because he cleaned, trimmed, emptied the trash, and gave the entire building it's image to the public. I wanted them to know that they were very important and were appreciated.

One of the guys said, "*Hey lady, what makes you so different?*"

I simply responded, "*I have a personal relationship with Jesus Christ, and He has taught me that I am to do unto others as I would have people do unto me.*"

As a result of that meeting, the guys at the courthouse began doing a much better job with their own work. They seemed to enjoy their jobs a lot more as they now felt valued and respected.

When you live under the umbrella of respect, you raise the quality of life for each person you meet. As you seek to build others, you cannot help but to build yourself in the process.

People who respect others feel secure. Unfortunately, some people feel the need to put others down in order to feel secure about themselves. But disrespecting others is the quickest way to show insecurity and weakness of self. Disrespect is at the heart of all racism, sexual abuse, substance abuse, violence, hatred, and fear. Whether you chose to respect or disrespect others, your decision will ultimately come back to you. By choosing respect, you become a positive change agent for your school, home, church, and community.

Respect Without Conditions

During the Vietnam War, a story circulated about a soldier and the letters he was exchanging with his mother who was thousands of miles away at home.

He was said to have written, *"Mom, I was granted the leave of absence. They are going to let me come home for a month. I can't wait to see you."*

She wrote back, "*Son, I am going to fix your favorite meals, get your bedroom ready, and throw a party for you with all your friends. I cannot wait to see you, either!*"

The son responded, "*Mom, I was wondering. Could I have one of my buddies come home with me? He and I have been through several battles together and he is very important to me.*"

She wrote back, "*Son, any buddy of yours is a buddy of mine. Tell him that he is welcome to stay the whole month; I will fix up the spare bedroom for him. Looking forward to you coming home.*"

He then replied, "*Mom, thanks for letting my buddy come with me. One thing though, in one of our battles he lost an arm and he is a little sensitive and wants to know if he can still come home with me.*"

The mother answered, "*Son, tell your friend that he can come and stay for two weeks, but not the whole time. I hope that you understand. Looking forward to seeing you.*"

The son wrote again and said, "*Mom, it is only a few days until I see you. I forgot to tell you, but my buddy not only lost his arm, but he lost both of his legs as well. Can he still come home? He is self conscious about it and wanted me to make sure that it was okay.*"

She felt compelled to answer, "*Son, I have all the food purchased, your room is cleaned and I have sent the invitations out to your friends for the party. We are so excited about you coming home. But about your friend, I don't think bringing him with you would be a very good idea. I hope that you will understand, but I have a reputation to uphold in this town and having a person here with an arm and two legs missing would be embarrassing. Plus, I am not sure how I could take care of a 'stump.'"*

Government officials delivered the next letter that the mother received, with a knock on her door. They handed her the envelope and she opened it. It read:

"We deeply regret to inform you that your son is dead. He did not die in battle. He did not die in war. Your son committed suicide.

Please be at the airport at the specified date and time to identify the body."

The mother cried, *"Why, why? He was so close to coming home. Why did he kill himself?"* She went to the airport on the appointed day and time. The plane landed and began to unload a coffin with an American Flag draped over it. They brought it before her and began to unlatch the locks on the coffin. When they lifted up the lid of the coffin for her to identify her son, she screamed, *"My God! My God! What have I done?"*

There lay her son with one arm and two legs missing. The young man's letters were obviously not about a handicapped friend but about himself. He wanted to know if he would be loved, accepted, and respected in the less-than-perfect condition the war had left him in. His mother came to the shocking realization that it was her conditional respect—not his injuries—that had led to his death.

Disrespect can kill a person's self-esteem and leave deep, emotional wounds. Disrespect tears at the core of humanity. The very moment you chose to live and operate under the umbrella of respect for all, you will take a giant leap towards the elimination of racism, hate, violence, fear, abuse, and even death!

Our Own Calcutta

A few years ago I had the opportunity to personally meet Mother Teresa, of Calcutta. She was a great humanitarian and a Nobel Peace Prize winner. Through her work and words, I learned a great deal. Mother Teresa helped me to see that although it is impossible to respect everyone we meet, it is possible to *treat* everyone we meet with respect.

Mother Teresa once said to me, "*In my country, when people hunger for bread, we give them a piece of bread, and they hunger no more. In your country, people hunger for love, but it is not given freely. Your hunger is worse than ours is. Go back to your own Calcutta and be Jesus to your people.*"

Each of us lives in our *own Calcutta*—a place where we need to be valued, loved and respected. Are you willing to be a change agent by raising the quality of life for each person you meet? Open the umbrella of respect for all those around you. Be like Jesus to people in your *own Calcutta* by doing unto others, as you would have them do unto you!

Chapter

13

It's Time to
Come Home

by
BILL SANDERS

TEEN
POWER
Thru CHRIST

It's Time to Come Home

by
BILL SANDERS

E xcuses. Some people have excuses for everything. I recently saw the *Complete Book of Excuses* at the bookstore. It's sad when excuses keep us away from studying, getting a job, achieving at a sport, and not becoming the person we were intended to be. The worst excuses of all are those that keep people from getting to know the love of God.

If you ever hear these excuses why not try these comebacks:

Excuse: "I didn't go to church because I don't get any-thing out of it."

Answer: "Come to ours, we give out bulletins."

Excuse: "I don't read the Bible because I don't under-stand it."

Answer: "There are things I don't understand also, but that doesn't stop me from enjoying them. For instance, I don't understand how a chicken, cow, and sheep all eat grass. The chicken turns the grass into eggs, the cow turns it into milk, and the sheep turns it into wool. I don't understand it, but I still eat the eggs, drink the milk, and wear the wool."

Excuse: "There are too many hypocrites in church."

Answer #1: "Come anyway, one more won't matter."

#2: "If you let a hypocrite stand between you and God, that just means the hypocrite is a little closer to God than you are."

#3: "If you are hiding behind a hypocrite then you must be smaller than the hypocrite is or you couldn't hide behind him."

Excuse: "I don't have faith because I don't believe what I can't see."

Answer: "I don't understand nor can I see electricity, but I still turn on the lights when it's dark. Every time you put gas in your car it takes faith. Or eating yogurt. And what about grits? Actually that's where I draw the line! I don't eat things that MOVE!

All kidding aside, many people stay away from God for a stronger reason than excuses. Pain. They have been hurt and the natural thing to do for many people is to blame it on God.

Bob and Sue's Story

Bob and Sue both had alcoholic fathers and they each had a very rough childhood. They were drawn together because they were mad at the world together. They got pierced and tattooed together. They shook their fists at authority together. When they heard the story of Jesus, they were both seventeen years old. Tired of the angry and hopeless feelings inside, Bob asked Jesus to take over his life that very night. He asked Sue why she wouldn't give Jesus a try, and her answer was all too familiar to people like me who work with teens. She said, "I'm not going to trust any heavenly father with my heart, after what my earthly father has done with my life!"

Here is the interesting part. Bob's pain was just as deep. His childhood tears were just as sad and pitiful. His frightening nights were just as lonely. The difference between Bob and Sue was that he chose to turn *back to* God, instead of turning his back *on* God.

I say that Bob turned *back to* God because God has revealed himself to every person who has ever lived. Throughout each of our lives he tugs at our hearts to come to him, trust him, and to put our lives in his hands.

These verses show clearly that no one can use the excuse that they never knew of God. "For the truth about God is known to them (all people) instinctively; God has put this knowledge in their hearts. Since earliest times men have seen the earth and sky and all God made, and have known of his existence and great eternal power. So they will have no excuse when they stand before God at Judgment Day. Yes, they knew about him all right, but they wouldn't admit it or worship him or even thank him for all his daily care. Claiming themselves to be wise without God, they became utter fools instead" (Romans 1:19–20,22).

Every Person's Choice

Every person who has ever been hurt by another, especially a child by a parent, has a choice to make: to focus on the problem or to find a solution to the problem. The problem with problems is that the more you concentrate on them, the bigger they become. Anger, worry, and frustration also seem to multiply, pulling us deeper and deeper into a quicksand of mental turmoil.

How many teens do you know who have turned their backs on God because God never rescued them during their terrible time of need? Maybe they were abused as children, deeply hurt by their parents' divorce, made to be the black sheep of the family, or were given up for adoption. Other factors, such as not being able to talk to parents, parents expecting perfection, feeling as though you're not measuring up, and feeling guilty for not being a "good Christian" can be just as damaging.

This person I am describing might be you. If so, read on, because the rest of this chapter could literally save your life. If none of this describes you, get on your knees, thank God for your family, count your blessings, and share this with someone who could desperately use a double dose of God's love.

Bad Things and Good People

Have you ever wondered why bad things happen to good people? Most of us have asked this question at one time or another. When I hear of world disasters where thousands of innocent people are killed, I often wonder why God didn't do something to stop it. I even get more confused when I read where parents sexually abuse their children, beat them, abandon them, give them drugs, or lock them in a closet for months at a time.

When you are in need of truthful answers to life's most troubling questions, always go to the greatest life handbook ever made—the Bible. What does God have to say about good people and bad things?

Good People:

- "For all have sinned and fall short of the glory of God" (Romans 3:23).

- "There is none righteous, not even one" (Romans 3:10).

These two verses show us that every person who has ever lived has made mistakes and committed sins. That means that other than Jesus—the only sinless person—no one has ever truly been "good."

Bad Things:

• "And we know that God causes everything to work together for the good of those who love God and are called according to his purpose for them" (Romans 8:28).

Even though the first two verses show that "**good or perfect people**" do not exist, "**bad things**" certainly do. They are called sins. Evil is rampant in our world, causing scars, wrecked lives, and ruined families. Worst of all, when hurtful events occur, many people turn from God and toward Satan. Instead of moving closer to the One who helps with recovery, healing and forgiveness, they honor their enemy—the devil—by hanging on to bitterness, anger, revenge, and hatred. And what most people don't think of when they are in the eye of the storm of their painful situation is that the devil caused their pain in the first place.

Making Bad Things Good

When Romans 8:28 says that "God causes all things to work together for the good of those who love him," it means that God can help anyone who wants His help, to make sure that something good can come from something bad. The verse could be rewritten to say, "For anyone who loves the Lord Jesus and is trying their best to live for him, God is able to turn today's troubles into tomorrow's triumphs." Or it could read, "No matter what terrible thing has ever happened to you, if you will trust God, He will turn it into long-range good for you."

This doesn't mean that God caused the bad thing to happen. John 10:10 reveals the opposing roles of Satan and God when Jesus says, "the thief's (Satan) purpose is to steal and kill and destroy. My purpose is to give life in all its fullness."

Personally speaking, all of my childhood pain kept me from a friendship with God until I was twenty-seven. I was living out my anger and ruining nearly every relationship that was important to me. I hope and pray that you are much wiser than I was and that you do what ever it takes to get close and stay close to Jesus.

The Run-Away Puppy

Imagine getting a puppy for your birthday. It is beautiful and you love it to pieces. You take good care of it, feed it, and clean up after it. You think of it all day while you are at school and simply cannot wait to get home to see it, hold it and spend time with it.

A month later however, your puppy won't let you pet it, and every time you go near him, he growls at you. When you try to pick him up, he runs away and ends up living with a wild bunch of stray dogs that terrorize your town at night.

One day the neighbor lady tells you she saw a mean dog go in your yard, frightening your pup, holding it to the ground with its teeth sunk deep in your precious pup's throat. She also tells you that the very dog your pup left you for is the mean one that almost killed it in the first place.

You can't believe your ears. You are broken hearted. After all you did for the puppy, taking care of him, cleaning, feeding, and, most of all, loving him with your whole heart, he runs away from you. And he isn't even smart enough to see that the one that took him away from his warm, safe home and three square meals a day is the very one he has chosen to follow and be like.

One of your friends hears this story and tells you what a stupid ungrateful mutt it must be. The friend advises you to forget all about the puppy, and, if you do see him, to either shoot him or call the dog catcher. But those aren't your thoughts at all. Your hope and prayer is that one day your dog will do one simple thing; come home! You would be so glad to see him that you would forgive him, pet him, and play with him in such a comforting way that he would soon be healed of his emotional wounds and return to his joyful, normal self.

I imagine that's how God must feel like at times.

A Game of Survival?

In the TV show "Survival," everyday people were placed in a game where they had to do whatever they could to outlast the other contestants for a grand prize of one million dollars. They had very few ethical guidelines, so the contestants lied and cheated each other through out the lengthy game. As the contest came to a conclusion, the runners up made comments about the final two remaining players and then elected a winner. One woman was so angry that she insulted one of the finalists and then told her that if she ever saw this young woman lying on the side of the road dying, she would not even stop to help her. If you saw the show you will probably always remember those incredible words of anger and revenge.

Eric Harris and Dylan Klebold were so filled with inner turmoil and in such desperate need of attention that they wanted to inflict others with their pain. So they went on their deadly rampage at Columbine High School. Neither boy had the courage to turn to God or even to ask his parents for help. They lived out their own twisted episode of survival convinced of only one thing. Doom.

I spent twenty-seven years in a game of survival with the devil as my co-pilot, but I didn't realize it while it was happening. He led me down the wrong path and laughed at each head-on collision I made.

A Letter on the Pillow

Imagine coming home after school and finding this letter on your pillow.

Dear (Your name),

I have been waiting to talk to you all day. I thought for sure you would spend some time with me this morning when you got up, but you were too busy getting ready for school. Then just before the bus came, you sat down, and I was sure you would at least say "hi" or perhaps thank me for the sunrise, but instead you watched TV.

At lunch I was so thrilled to have you talk with me as you always do, but you were too embarrassed to pray, and you just started eating. I was hurt when I saw you cheat off another student's test.

After school I looked forward to being with you, but with sports and homework you flopped down in bed and fell fast asleep. It's OK; I will watch over you tonight and wait for you to come to me tomorrow. I love you so much. I have the answer to all of your questions, and I can fill all of your needs. Please come back and let me shower you with forgiveness, love and inner joy.

Love, Jesus

Even though a letter like that may never appear on your pillow, I believe that Jesus writes letters every bit as compelling on our hearts daily.

What are You Waiting For?

Jesus is waiting. His arms are wide open just as when He died for each of us on the cross. Let Him show you that He is a man of His word and will help you fulfill your every dream. Don't let another day go by with your eyes turned away from Him. Today is the day for salvation. Today is the day for your homecoming.

Here is a simple prayer that I prayed when I turned my life over to Jesus on Christmas day, 1978. You might want to pray something like it if you feel God tugging at your heart right now.

> "Dear Jesus, I don't know much about you or the Bible but I do know that I have really made a mess of my life. Please forgive me for all of my sins. I am tired of hurting others and myself and destroying so many relationships. I'm also sorry for the times I've hurt you. Please make my heart clean again. Take away my inner pain. Jesus, take over my life. I need you as my Savior, and I need you as my friend."

It doesn't really matter what words you use, just as long as you are sincere and mean it with all your heart.

Write or e-mail me if you ever need someone to talk to.

Jesus is whistling for all lost pups. He is waiting with open arms and a smile on his face. Run to him now.

Never forget:

There is nothing you can do to make God love you any more. And nothing you have done could get Him to love you any less.

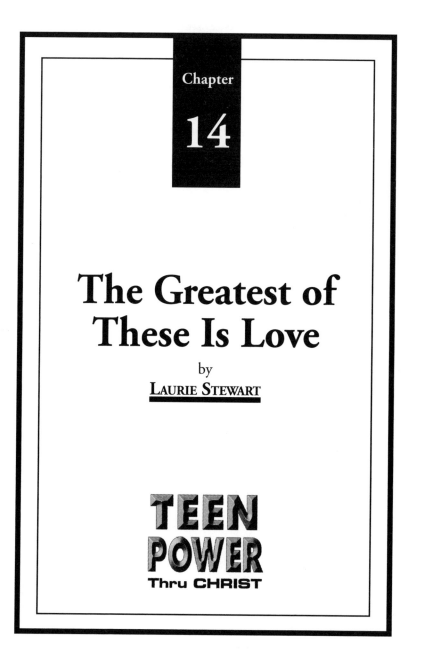

Chapter

14

The Greatest of These Is Love

by
LAURIE STEWART

TEEN POWER

Thru CHRIST

The Greatest of These Is Love

by
LAURIE STEWART

"Love the Lord your God with all your heart and with all your soul and with all your mind. This is the first and greatest commandment. And the second is like it: **"Love your neighbor as yourself"** *(Matthew 22:37–39, emphasis mine).*

* * * * *

We were created to serve an incredible purpose! Daily we are called to love God and to love others. According to God's Word, this is our reason for living! Through His love and His strength we are able to fulfill these awesome commands. By helping those in need and appreciating others, powerful teens express love for people and love for God.

Amy doesn't see with her eyes; she sees with her heart. Amy is blind. When I first met Amy, I was going through difficult times having to make decisions that would affect my entire life. One decision included breaking off a marriage engagement. Even though I knew breaking up was the right thing to do, I couldn't eat or sleep. I was so miserable that I didn't want to get out of bed in the morning. Finally, when I realized that I couldn't live life to the fullest with blankets pulled over my head, I decided to fill my waking hours with work. I became a workaholic.

One night Amy called and asked me to go shopping. Consumed with work and not really listening, I thought she meant shopping at the mall—that would take up too much of my time! I said, *"Amy, I can't. I've got to work. Thanks! Bye."* As I hung up the phone, I realized that perhaps she had wanted to go grocery shopping. After all, she couldn't see to drive! Feeling guilty for being so self-absorbed, I called her back. *"Amy did you mean grocery shopping?"*

She answered, *"Yes."*

Minutes later, I was on my way to Western Michigan University's campus housing. Entering Amy's apartment, I saw three blind girls singing and playing guitars—just like sighted girls. That's when it struck me how quickly we judge people! Outward appearance, skin color, hairstyle, and clothes are all things the sighted too easily judge. How different it is for the blind. They don't care about outward appearances. They only see what's in our hearts. That can be scary!

Amy invited one of her blind friends to come, and the three of us went shopping. With a girl on each arm, I pushed the cart through the aisles, identifying the contents of each shelf. I was challenged to describe objects that I always took for granted. How can you describe to a blind person the deep ruby red of an apple or the fuzzy brown skin of a kiwi? Never had I appreciated my eyesight until I had to see for three people. For two hours my focus was on helping others. An amazing thing happened—I totally forgot my personal struggles and helped make a difficult task for two blind girls into an enjoyable, blessed outing for all of us. Powerful teens seize opportunities to help others.

"Do nothing out of selfish ambition or vain conceit, but in humility consider others better than yourselves. Each of you should look not only to your own interests, but also to the interests of others . . . "
(Philippians 2:3–4)

We love and honor God when we love others! Powerful teens live their God-ordained purpose by looking for ways to love and bring people together.

The Love of Leon

I first met Leon when I was training a group of student leaders, and he definitely stood out from the crowd. Tall and lanky, he participated with enthusiasm and humor. He sat in the front row, always ready for action. The final two hours of the training that focused on respecting and appreciating others were the most powerful. By the power of the Holy Spirit, the students received the message; we connected!

After I finished speaking, Leon hugged and thanked me. He was so inspired, he asked his advisor if the students could stand and verbally thank each other after the break, but he was told that *there just wasn't time.* Still, I admired his tenacity, his confidence, and his willingness to seize the moment.

During the following eighteen months, Leon and I talked frequently over the phone. He told me he wanted to be a full-time pastor and speaker. He'd already had many anointed experiences ministering and speaking. Each time we talked I felt uplifted. Leon told me about the hours he spent in the middle of the night praying, interceding, and talking with God. He shared the importance of protecting his closeness and fellowship with his Lord. He avoided places where he felt he would be tempted to disobey God. He spoke often of his godly, prayerful mom and how she inspired him to be Christ-like. He so admired her. Our conversations were always deep and spiritual. I had no doubt in my heart that Leon would become an incredibly anointed preacher.

Over the next few months, I fell out of contact with Leon. It seemed that I had gotten too busy and *didn't have time* to return his calls as quickly as I should have. When I did get back to him, I would usually miss him. Leon wasn't offended and continued to call my office. One of his last calls concerned a friend whom Leon felt needed help. He left a message and said he'd write for suggestions; I never got his letter . . .

Within the same time period, Leon told a friend that he hadn't seen his aunts, uncles, and cousins since he was very little. He felt that his family had grown apart and he decided to do something about it. He began to organize a big family reunion celebration scheduled for the 4th of July. He called all of his relatives, but they each told Leon that *they didn't have time* for a reunion.

Two weeks before the date of the canceled reunion, Leon was killed in a train crash. At the funeral, the entire family was together again but not for the joyous celebration for which Leon had hoped. The following year on July 4th, Leon's family did have the kind of reunion Leon had wanted. *They made the time.*

Leon was an excellent example of love. My personal definition of Leon is: *On fire for God, full of life, a risk-taker, compassionate, hard-working, obedient to God, conversationalist, wise, and Holy Spirit filled.* He lived up to this definition, bringing people together and bringing them to God, and he accomplished this even in death. When I think of Leon, I think of a true Christian who had his priorities in line:

God—1st

Family—2nd

Work—3rd

Leon knew he was called to be God's vessel. He stepped aside and invited God to work through him. God most certainly did! Powerful teens live their God-given purpose by loving others and uniting people together in love. **"If we walk in the light, as he is in the light, we have fellowship with one another . . . "** (1 John 1:7). Powerful teens know they can live out their God-given purpose *__now!__* **"Don't let anyone look down on you because you are young, but set an example for the believers in speech, in life, in love, in faith and in purity . . . "** (1 Timothy 4:12).

Powerful teens also demonstrate love by encouraging others; they are "quick" to show their appreciation:

Love and Encouragement in Cowboy Boots

As a college student, one of my most powerful influences was Chuck McCarter, an enthusiastic Texan who loved his southern heritage. Chuck was 100% authentic, and to show it he wore cowboy boots everywhere. During Tuesday night basketball games at the church, he would kick off his Reeboks and wear his cowboy boots on the gym floor. Imagine seeing a full grown man—with exposed snow white legs—doing lay-ups in cowboy boots!

Chuck was a loving husband and father. He was faithful, godly, healthy, and successful. At age thirty-eight and in search of a challenge, Chuck decided to go back to college. Every day he saw me, he gave me a huge hug and asked how I was doing. He had—and used—the gift of encouragement, and I always felt better after being in the vicinity of Chuck McCarter. He gave, he cared, he loved.

Four years went by, and Chuck had made it through all his college courses. The Monday before he was scheduled to graduate, I walked upstairs to the room where Chuck was supposed to be taking his "final" final exam. (He had always encouraged and appreciated me, so I finally decided this would be my chance to surprise him, give him a hug and tell him how much I appreciated him.) I peeked into his classroom, but I didn't see Chuck. "*He should be here!*" I thought. "*Where could he possibly be?*" The next day, I learned the terrible truth.

The day of his last test, Chuck had gone in for his annual medical checkup. Within the first five minutes of his physical exam, Chuck had suffered a heart attack and had died in the doctor's office. I could not believe it! Why did this happen so suddenly? Why was I robbed of my chance to tell Chuck how much I appreciated him in my life and how much his encouragement meant to me? I was in total shock!

I avoided the Tuesday night basketball league for the entire year that followed, but I decided to go to the last game of the season. As I got out of the car and walked toward the gym, I felt as though I had been hit by a huge boulder. Everything was the same as it had always been: same gym, same people, same uniforms. The only thing that was different was that I knew I would not see Chuck.

A deep sadness came over me. Although I felt like turning away from the gymnasium doors and running home, something stopped me. My head echoed the powerful words I had heard another speaker say: "*Successful people do the things unsuccessful people dislike doing and will not do.*"

Immediately I thought of Romans 8:28, "*And we know that in all things God works for the good of those who love him, who have been called according to his purpose.*"

Although it would have been easier to turn and run, I knew God wanted me to face the situation and to learn from the pain. God wanted me to use Chuck's example to learn how I could encourage others in my chosen profession of speaking to youth.

Instead of leaving, I sat down on the bleachers, took out my pen and paper, and wrote a few simple words:

Chuck

1. enjoyed life.

2. appreciated people.

3. gave hugs.

I immediately felt better and started to watch the game when Ed walked in. If you've ever known someone so peppy, so motivated, and so enthusiastic that you'd like to wring their neck and say, "*Will you have one bad day, please?*" then you know Ed. He walked over to me, sat down, and jabbed me in the ribs. With his fifteen year old, lopsided grin he asked, "*How ya doin', Laurie?*"

"*I keep thinking about Chuck,*" I answered.

Still smiling, Ed replied, "*I will always remember Chuck McCarter—when I'm a junior, when I'm a senior, when I go to college, when I get a job, when I hopefully get married and have kids, even when I'm a grandpa—**I will always remember** Chuck McCarter. He taught me three things:*

1. to enjoy life.

2. to appreciate people.

3. to give hugs."

That's what Ed said, **word for word**! I looked at him and said: "*You've been reading over my shoulder!*" (He didn't know what I was talking about.) I pulled out the piece of paper I had just written with those exact same three things on it and showed it to him.

We looked at each other and smiled. We knew we received a blessing by knowing a person who *daily* remembered to live out his godly purpose, someone who loved others and loved God!

A couple of years later, I visited Chuck's grave. In the upper left corner of his tombstone was a cross. Chuck had a strong, firm faith in Jesus Christ. Engraved in the lower right hand corner was a pair of cowboy boots! Below that it read: "*With a delightful drawl he lived with love, compassion, and understanding for all.*"

What About You?

Powerful teens remember that their ultimate purpose in life is to love God and love others. Through God's grace they are thankful for God's blessings, they encourage, and they appreciate others! **"Therefore encourage one another and build each other up . . . "** (1 Thessalonians 5:11).

Is there someone you need to encourage, appreciate, or forgive? Please don't wait, as I did. Write a letter of encouragement and appreciation. Make that call, send that card, or initiate that visit!

Name of Person: _____

Action: _____

Date: _____

My Prayer for You

I pray that you have been blessed and encouraged to live out your God-given purpose. God loves you! He wants to bless you with a life of abundance. His purpose for your life is far better than you could ever imagine!

> *"Love the Lord your God with all your heart*
> *and with all your soul and with all your mind.*
> *This is the first and greatest commandment.*
> *And the second is like it:*
> *Love your neighbor as yourself."*
> (Matthew 22:37–39)

When we live out God's plan, our lives are filled with peace, love, and hope. Blessings to you as you live your life as a *"Child of the King!"*

ACTION STEPS:

1. Every day count at least five blessings. Think "thankful."

2. Each day repeat, "My purpose for living today is to love God and to love others." Remind yourself of this throughout the day. God will give you the strength and the ability to love others. Ask Him! (Matthew 22:37–39)

3. Say something nice to or about another person. Smile at as many people as you can! (Psalm 19:14)

4. Once a week send a card, a small gift, or a note of appreciation to someone. Make this a habit!

5. Read the Bible daily. Focus on the truths of the Bible. (2 Peter 1:3–4)

6. Repeat Philippians 4:13: "I can do everything through Him who gives me strength" five times before getting out of bed each morning. Memorize scriptures. (Powerful verses to memorize are: Matthew 22:37–39, Zechariah 7:9–10, 1 Thessalonians 5:11, and 1 Thessalonians 5:13–15.)

7. Daily ask God to control your words, your heart, and your thoughts. When ungodly thoughts enter your mind, ask God to replace them with pure, positive,

and loving thoughts. Pray: "Lord, help me to see this person with your eyes." (Psalm 139:23–24 and Philippians 4:8)

8. Make yourself available to help those in need. Volunteer at a homeless shelter, nursing home . . . (Matthew 25:35–40).

PRAY THIS WITH ME:

Dear Heavenly Father:

I surrender myself to You and to Your purpose for my life. God I ask that you mold me and change me into the likeness of Your Son, Jesus. God break down all the barriers in my heart that keep me from loving you and loving others. Please change me, Lord, so that I may love others unconditionally as you have loved me.

In Jesus Name,
Amen

Meet the
Authors

TEEN POWER
Thru CHRIST

Eric Chester & Generation Why
1410 Vance Street – Ste. #201
Lakewood, CO 80215
303-239-9999
Fax: 303-239-9901
www.ericchester.com
eric@ericchester.com

ERIC CHESTER

Call him crazy, zany, or downright weird; but one thing is certain . . . when Eric talks—teens respond and take positive action! Eric is a former teacher, coach, sports promoter, and television talk show host. Since 1989, his entertaining multimedia conference keynotes and school assemblies have been enjoyed by over a million students from throughout the world. Eric's student-oriented keynotes and workshops tackle the tough issues today's teens face including: motivation, self-esteem, peer pressure, healthy choices, character, respect, and leadership. Eric and his wife Lori have four teenagers and live in Lakewood, Colorado.

Bill Cordes
2920 Quivira
Great Bend, KS 67530
316-793-7227
Toll Free: 800-401-6670
Fax: 316-793-5024
www.billcordes.com
yogowypi@aol.com

BILL CORDES

Bill Cordes loves Christ and loves his wife Karla and their children Josha, Shannon, and Easton. He lives in the "hood"—parenthood— and is a member of the Green Eggs and Ham Gang. When not with his family, Bill speaks to teens, parents, teachers, college students, and businesses with audiences totaling nearly one million people in 39 states across the United States. In his programs, Bill combines humor, life experience, participation, and tons of tools for building successful lives. He contributed to *Teen Power Too*, *Teen EmPower*, and *Lead Now or Step Aside*.

JOHN CRUDELE

John Crudele Productions
6100 Green Valley Drive, Suite 120
Minneapolis, MN 55438
952-835-0008
Toll Free 800-899-9543
Fax: 952-835-0004
www.johncrudele.com
john@johncrudele.com

John is a compelling speaker for school, conference, church, and association events. For 15 years, his humorous insights and powerful delivery style have propelled him to deliver more than 3500 programs to over a million youth, teachers, and parents internationally, to be a frequent TV guest, and to host his own national radio talk show. With compassion and conviction, John addresses sensitive youth and family topics and destructive societal issues. Audiences are moved by his stories, attracted to his authenticity, and challenged by his honesty. John's books include *Making Sense of Adolescence: How to Parent From the Heart* and contributions to the *TEEN POWER* series.

KEN DAVIS

Ken Davis Productions
P.O. Box 745940
Arvada, CO 80006-5940
303-425-1319
Fax: 303-420-0764
www.kendavis.com
info@kendavis.com

It is hard to describe Ken Davis. He is an award-winning author of 9 books. He is a comedian, speaker, and entertainer who is widely recognized by his entire family. He is the president of Dynamic Communicators International, a company dedicated to equipping communicators to prepare with focus, deliver with clarity and speak with power. Most important he the husband of Diane, the dad of two grown children and the love-crazed grandfather of Kialee Brielle. Ken has dedicated his life to using his gifts to tell the world of the power available through Christ.

SAM GLENN

Youth For Success
608 S. Washington Street – Ste. 101
Naperville, IL 60540
317-776-2890
Toll Free: 800-818-6378
Fax: 630-375-1856
www.youth4success.com
www.makefootprints.com

As a nationally recognized speaker who addresses youth groups, schools and Corporations all over America, Sam's personal mission is to inspire people of all ages to squeeze the best out of life. Not really sure what do with his life after college, Sam went from a job as a janitor to speaking for the Billy Graham crusades. He has spoken to crowds as large as 80,000 in the Pontiac Silverdome and has addressed close to a million people in the last two years. The radical impact of Sam's message gets people fired up about living life to the fullest!

DOUG HERMAN

ReaLife Presentations
PO Box 270510
Littleton, CO 80127-0010
303-973-4758
Toll Free: 888-973-4758
www.dougherman.com
doug@dougherman.com

Doug's audiences find themselves laughing through their tears. His first book *Faith Quake* shares his powerful journey—the loss of a wife and daughter to AIDS from a blood transfusion. He's spoken nationally in churches, schools and conferences and has conducted over 1000 assemblies to over 1 million teens on the topic of sexual abstinence. He has appeared on *Focus On The Family*, *Life Outreach with James Robison*, and *100 Huntley Street*. He's written for *FaithMD*, *ParentLife*, *Living With Teenagers*, *Leadership Journal*, and *Youthworker*. Make him your friend and take him diving or golfing! He lives in Littleton, Colorado with his wife Stephanie and three children.

JAY LAFFOON

Jay Laffoon
PO Box 93
Alma, MI 48801
517-466-5574
Fax: 517-463-5572
www.jaylaffoon.com
Jay@comresources.org

For twenty years, Jay Laffoon has been communicating Jesus to audiences of all ages, sizes, and backgrounds. His versatile speaking skills deliver clarity and power to every event. Jay's humor, story telling, and genuine delivery make the truth burst alive as he speaks. Jay's track record shows his commitment to seeing lost souls won for Christ. His adaptable speaking style is great for all settings. Whether speaking at a school assembly program, retreat, or conference, or to a business management team, Jay's enthusiasm leaves an indelible mark on his listeners.

BOB LENZ

Life Promotions
213 E. College Ave.
Appleton, WI 54911
Toll Free: 800-955-5433
Fax: 920-738-5587
www.lifepromotions.com
Speaking@lifepromotions.com

"I don't want to see young people cheated out of life."

Bob is the founder of Life Promotions, a ministry committed to reaching youth with the Gospel. Through public school assembly programs, Bob, with the aid of musical acts and illusionists, presents a message of hope, courage and respect. The program is designed to draw youth out to an evening rally where the Gospel is preached, lives are changed, and youth meet Christ. Although Bob loves speaking, his first commitment is to his wife, Carol, and their five children.

ELLEN MARIE

Youth Support, Inc.
P.O. Box 22665
Minneapolis, MN 55422-0665
763-529-6884
Fax: 763-529-3187
youthspt@aol.com

Ellen has been speaking professionally on relationships and sexual abstinence since 1992 and is a member of the National Speakers Association. She holds a Masters Degree, is a former director of a teen pregnancy center, and is a co-author of *Teen Power Too* and *Lead Now . . . Or Step Aside!* When speaking, Ellen uses humor and audience interaction as she shares unforgettable stories causing teens to seriously consider the consequences of their choices. Ellen has been featured as guest expert on the television talk shows *Montel Williams, Ricki Lake,* and *Life on the Rock*, as well as numerous radio programs.

BOBBY PETROCELLI

10 Seconds, Inc.
P.O. Box 923
Bellport, NY 11713
Toll Free: 800-547-7933
Fax: 631-286-7677
www.10seconds.org
tseconds@aol.com

The greatest compliment that a young person can pay you is that you are REAL! That's the term young people use when describing Bobby Petrocelli—REAL. Bobby's source for being REAL is his Hero, Jesus, whom he has been serving since he was seven years old! He gives all the credit to his Lord and savior Jesus Christ for getting him through an unbelievable tragedy in his life. Through his organization, 10 Seconds, Inc., Bobby is a "man on a mission"—to bring faith, hope and love to all who hear him.

TERRY PRISK

Real. Practical. Genuine. Sincere. These words describe Terry Prisk's speaking and writing. Terry's goal is to make Biblical truths come alive in his writings and presentations. His heart is to see students reach their full potential, making the spiritual area of their lives the driving force behind their social, physical, and mental development. He loves being around students, sharing with them and their families, and helping them grow in their daily walk with Christ. God has given him an ability to communicate to groups—small and large, young and old. Terry, his wife, and their four children reside in Highland, Michigan.

Contemporary Communication
P .O. Box 506
Highland, MI 48357
248-887-8977
Fax: 248-889-2442
www.terryprisk.com
terryprisk@aol.com

LORI SALIERNO

"Lady, you made a difference in our school today," a tough guy said to Lori after she spoke at a school assembly. The week before, the boy had come to class with a loaded gun. Lori's positive attitude and contagious spirit help students build self-esteem and confidence about the future. Whether she is speaking on sexual purity at a rally, leading a group as they trek through the Andes mountains, or addressing policy makers in Washington, D.C., Lori's message is loud and clear: "Get out of the comfort zone and join God's current!" Passion burns within Lori's souls for students—everyone from junior high through college. Her goal is to see the cause of Christian service advance among our young generations. She is the author of *Designed for Excellence* and *When Roosters Crow*. Lori is the Founder and Executive Officer of Celebrate Life International, Inc. She lives in Atlanta, Georgia with her handsome husband, Kurt.

Celebrate Life International
6060 Lake Acworth Dr., Suite N
Acworth, GA 30101
770-529-7700
Fax 770-529-7711
www.CelebrateLife.org
cli@CelebrateLife.org

BILL SANDERS

Bill Sanders can't hit a golf ball as well as Tiger Woods, but he can hold a high school audience in the palm of his hand for over an hour! He personally answers a thousand letters each year and has authored 14 teen and parent books. Bill is featured in *Chicken Soup for the Teenage Soul* and has shared the stage with Presidents Ford and Reagan. He is committed to his wife and three teens and will work just as hard for your school or meeting as he did on his first speech in 1978.

Bill Sanders
8495 Valleywood Ln.
Portage, MI 49024
616-323-8074
Fax: 616-323-9180
www.billspeaks.com
billspeaks@juno.com

LAURIE STEWART

Laurie Stewart, CSP, is a nationally known speaker. She's considered an expert in human relations and school climate improvement, attitudinal development, and communication skills. Since 1983, Laurie has presented staff development programs, assemblies, keynotes, leadership training, and parent talks throughout the United States and Canada. Laurie has authored a book and audio-tape programs, *The Winning School: The Team Approach to Healthy School Climate* and *Finding My Faith*. She's a graduate of Western Michigan University and has earned the Certified Speaking Professional designation through the National Speakers Association. Laurie's goal is to increase respect, faith, and appreciation in our society.

L.A. Stewart Presentations
P.O. Box 50869
Kalamazoo, MI 49005-0869
616-372-3200
Fax: 616-372-3203
lastewart@compuserve.com

If you liked TEEN POWER Thru CHRIST you'll love these other great books from ChesPress Publications

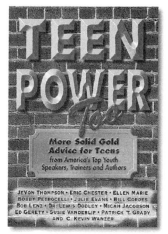

The Ultimate Handbook
for Student Leaders

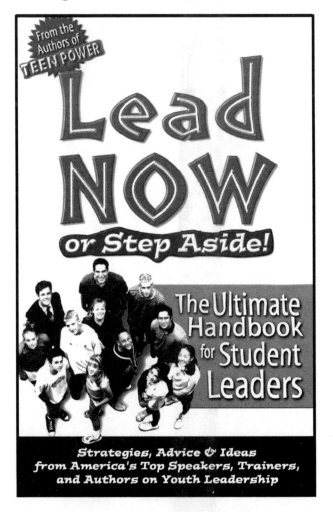

From the Authors of **TEEN POWER**

Lead
NOW
or Step Aside!

The Ultimate Handbook for Student Leaders

Strategies, Advice & Ideas
from America's Top Speakers, Trainers,
and Authors on Youth Leadership

Visit us on the web at
www.leadnowbook.com